Tongues

Scriptural Answers to Common Objections

Tongues

Scriptural Answers to Common Objections

By

David M. Pizzimenti

Albury Publishing
Tulsa, Oklahoma

Unless otherwise noted, all Scripture quotations are from the *King James Version* of the Bible.

The Scripture quotation marked AMP is taken from *The Amplified New Testament*. Copyright © 1958, 1987 by The Lockman Foundation, La Habra, California.

Tongues: Scriptural Answers to Common Objections
ISBN 1-88008-999-8
Copyright © 1996 by David M. Pizzimenti
Glory to Him Fellowship
AKA David Pizzimenti Ministries
P. O. Box 1289
Ozark, Alabama 36360

Published by ALBURY PUBLISHING
P.O. 470406
Tulsa, Oklahoma 74147-0406

Cover Art: The Pentecost by Van Der Werff

Dedication

To my darling wife, Kelly, and my two children, Jessica and Joshua. I never cease to thank our Lord for giving you to me to enrich my life.

Thank you, Kelly and Jessica, for all the typing that went into the production of this book.

Thank you also, Irma Townsend, for all of your skillful work in editing my teachings.

I would be remiss if I didn't thank Kenneth E. Hagin for the remarkable impact he has had in my life. First Corinthians 4:15 says, **For though ye have ten thousand instructors in Christ, yet have ye not many fathers.** Thank you "Dad" for your commitment and the lifelong dedication you have demonstrated in your ministry. Your life and ministry stand as an example of the faithfulness of God.

Contents

Chapter One
Bible Answers to Eight
Common Objections

All scripture is given by inspiration of God, and is profitable for doctrine, for reproof, for correction, for instruction in righteousness:

That the man of God may be perfect, throughly furnished unto all good works.

2 Timothy 3:16,17

If you are like me, when you first became born again, you did not know very much about the Bible. My initial interpretation of verse 16 proves how very little I knew. This verse was actually scary to me. I thought it meant the Bible needed to be corrected once in a while! Have you ever thought anything silly like that?

Because of my erroneous thinking, I stayed away from this verse for a long time. When I tried to talk to people about the Lord, they would say that the Bible is full of mistakes. I thought, "Yeah, but they have been corrected."

But as I grew in the Lord, I learned what verse 16 meant. **All scripture is given by inspiration of God** means the Bible is supernaturally written. The Bible was inspired by God Himself, and because of that, the Scripture is *profitable to you and me for biblical doctrine* or teaching.

Scripture is good for *reproof and correction*. The way you and I live and think needs to be reproved and corrected from time to time. Ideas we have about certain doctrines need to be reproved and corrected, based on what the Bible teaches about these doctrines.

Scripture is for *instruction in righteousness*. We need to learn what Scripture says about righteousness so we can put away sin-consciousness and enjoy our right standing with God.

When we allow the knowledge of the Word of God to teach us through life, we become more skillful in the *good works* of God. We also become partakers of His truth and wisdom in our spiritual lives.

I have chosen verse 16 of 2 Timothy 3 as a text because what I am about to discuss, speaking in other tongues, is scriptural. However, very often people make *not so scriptural* objections to this scriptural experience. I need to have a starting point, and this verse, I believe, is a point where every evangelical can agree.

The Bible must be the Christian's final authority on any topic. It is the Bible that was given by inspiration of God. Your denomination is not necessarily inspired of God. Your church, or former church, is not necessarily inspired by God. Your opinion, or former opinion, may have been inspired by well-meaning Bible teachers or church traditions, but you and I both know that the Bible is inspired by God. Therefore, we can use the Bible as our final say-so in any matter.

When talking about being filled with the Holy Ghost, I learned something long ago. If a person has legitimately made up their mind that they are not going to believe in this experience (speaking in other tongues when filled with the Holy Ghost) do not waste your time, or theirs, by having a Bible trivia debate with them. They will say, "My mind is made up. Don't confuse me with the facts." There is no sense battling with such a person to get them to believe.

In Matthew 5:6, Jesus said it like this, **Blessed are they which do hunger and thirst after righteousness: for they shall be filled.** If you are not thirsty or hungry, you will not be filled. Speaking in tongues will not catch you off guard. If you are not thirsty and hungry, no one can make you thirsty; no one can make you hungry. The desire for us to have all that God has available must grow from the inside of us. We have to become thirsty and hungry after the good things of God.

In Mark 16:17 Jesus said, **And these signs shall follow them that believe; In my name shall they cast out devils; they shall speak with new tongues.** One sign that follows the believer is *speaking with new tongues*. The flip side of this is, if you do not believe, you will not speak with tongues.

Scripture is not designed to persuade people who have made up their minds that this experience is not for them. Rather, it is designed to bless believers who want the truth. Experience has taught me that accepting misinterpreted Scripture, or putting faith in man's opinions, can create an obstacle or hindrance for believers who attempt to take the next step in their relationship with Jesus Christ.

The following pages in this chapter are dedicated to the sharing of eight objections some people have about speaking in other tongues. Some of the eight are twisted Scripture while others have no biblical basis whatsoever. There is no rank or order to these objections.

Objection One:
Speaking in Tongues Is of the Devil

Speaking in tongues is of the devil. Sometimes people say, "Well, those people are not speaking in tongues. They are speaking in demonic gibberish. Some demon gets on them and rants and raves." Or they say, "You are demon possessed," or, "Tongues are strictly from the devil." They believe this experience passed away when the writing of the Bible was completed.

Man's opinion that tongues are of the devil has no scriptural basis whatsoever. There is, however, a scriptural answer for this objection. When talking with anyone who is sincere about speaking in tongues, you will be able to open your Bible and have a discourse with them.

Some people want to be filled with the Holy Ghost with the evidence of speaking in other tongues but are afraid to respond to an altar call where hands will be laid on them. They are nervous, fearing maybe they will get a demon or maybe the devil will take advantage of them. In the Scripture Jesus gave an answer that will dispel all fear and apprehension:

> **And I say unto you, Ask, and it shall be given you; seek, and ye shall find; knock, and it shall be opened unto you.**
>
> **For every one that asketh receiveth; and he that seeketh findeth; and to him that knocketh it shall be opened.**
>
> **Luke 11:9,10**

We have always stopped reading at the end of verse 10 and said that Jesus was talking about prayer. But prayer was not the only subject about which Jesus was talking in this passage of Scripture. As a matter of fact, Jesus was not finished talking at the end of verse 10. If you have a fancy Bible, the red print which signifies Jesus as the speaker, continues after verse 10:

> **If a son shall ask bread of any of you that is a father, will he give him a stone? or if he ask a fish, will he for a fish give him a serpent?**
>
> **Luke 11:11**

Let's stop here for a moment and take a quick side journey. I think Jesus knew what was going to happen in the future, that the symbol of Christianity for the early Church would be the *fish*. In the first days of the Church, people were not allowed to draw crosses due to persecution of Christians. Instead, they would draw a fish symbol to show what they believed. Therefore, the fish became a symbol of Christianity. In the Greek, this symbol represented the crucifixion and resurrection.

Notice again in verse 11 of Luke 11 how Jesus contrasted a fish representing Himself and a serpent representing the devil: **...if he ask for a fish, will he for a fish give him a serpent?** If you ask for the Holy Ghost, He certainly is not going to give you a demon instead.

> **Or if he shall ask an egg, will he offer him a scorpion?**
>
> **If ye then, being evil, know how to give good gifts unto your children: how much more shall your heavenly Father give the Holy Spirit to them that ask him?**
>
> **Luke 11:12,13**

In this passage of Scripture, Jesus personally guarantees that you cannot ask for the Holy Spirit and receive a demon. Either it simply cannot happen or Jesus lied. I certainly do not believe Jesus lied. Do you? There is absolutely no scriptural basis to support the objection that speaking in tongues is of the devil. However, when people hear this objection over and over, they become frightened and nervous. They want to receive the Holy Ghost but are worried of receiving something that is not from God.

When you meet people with this fear, read and explain Luke 11:9-13 to them. Jesus personally said that if you ask for an egg, you will not get a scorpion. If you ask for bread, you will not get a stone. Accordingly, if you ask for the Holy Spirit, you will not get a demon.

Let's look at another element of this unscriptural objection:

> **Then was brought unto him one possessed with a devil, blind, and dumb: and he healed him, insomuch that the blind and dumb both spake and saw.**

And all the people were amazed, and said, Is not this the son of David?

But when the Pharisees heard it, they said, This fellow doth not cast out devils, but by Beelzebub the prince of the devils.

And Jesus knew their thoughts, and said unto them, Every kingdom divided against itself is brought to desolation; and every city or house divided against itself shall not stand:

And if Satan cast out Satan, he is divided against himself; how shall then his kingdom stand?

And if I by Beelzebub cast out devils, by whom do your children cast them out? therefore they shall be your judges.

But if I cast out devils by the Spirit of God, then the kingdom of God is come unto you.

Or else how can one enter into a strong man's house, and spoil his goods, except he first bind the strong man? and then he will spoil his house.

He that is not with me is against me; and he that gathereth not with me scattereth abroad.

Wherefore I say unto you, All manner of sin and blasphemy shall be forgiven unto men: but the blasphemy against the Holy Ghost shall not be forgiven unto men.

And whosoever speaketh a word against the Son of man, it shall be forgiven him: but whosoever speaketh against the Holy Ghost, it shall not be forgiven him, neither in this world, neither in the world to come.

Either make the tree good, and his fruit good; or else make the tree corrupt, and his fruit corrupt: for the tree is known by his fruit.

O generation of vipers, how can ye, being evil, speak good things? for out of the abundance of the heart the mouth speaketh.

Matthew 12:22-34

Religious people who were teachers of God's people began to get jealous of Jesus. They did not like the fact that the spotlight was on Jesus and off of them. They were being shown up by Him, the new preacher in town.

They also did not like how people were being drawn to Jesus saying, "This must be the Messiah." The religious leaders tried to deceive His followers by saying that what He was doing was by the power of Satan. You and I both know that what Jesus did was done by the power of the Holy Ghost.

> **How God anointed Jesus of Nazareth with the Holy Ghost and with power: who went about doing good, and healing all that were oppressed of the devil; for God was with him.**
>
> **Acts 10:38**

Because Jesus is merciful, He took time to teach these religious people that a kingdom divided against itself would not stand. He took time to show these so-called *teachers of the Law* that the entire premise of their argument was ludicrous. Additionally, he let them know that acts performed by Him were done by the power of the Holy Ghost.

After teaching them what was correct, Jesus issued a solemn warning: *To attribute the work of the Holy Ghost to a satanic manifestation was to blaspheme God's Holy Spirit.* This still applies today to those who know the Word, but choose to say that speaking in tongues is of the devil. These people are guilty of blasphemy. According to *Webster's Dictionary*, when one is guilty of blasphemy, they have insulted, shown contempt or lack of reverence for God. The following Scripture records this truth:

> **Verily I say unto you, All sins shall be forgiven unto the sons of men, and blasphemies wherewith soever they shall blaspheme:**

> But he that shall blaspheme against the Holy Ghost hath never forgiveness, but is in danger of eternal damnation:
>
> Because they said, He hath an unclean spirit.
> **Mark 3:28-30**

The Holy Ghost is not an unclean spirit. He is a holy, godly, clean Spirit.

> And whosoever shall speak a word against the Son of man, it shall be forgiven him: but unto him that blasphemeth against the Holy Ghost it shall not be forgiven.
> **Luke 12:10**

> Of how much sorer punishment, suppose ye, shall he be thought worthy, who hath trodden under foot the Son of God, and hath counted the blood of the covenant, wherewith he was sanctified, an unholy thing, and hath done despite unto the Spirit of grace?
>
> For we know him that hath said, Vengeance belongeth unto me, I will recompense, saith the Lord. And again, the Lord shall judge his people.
>
> It is a fearful thing to fall into the hands of the living God.
> **Hebrews 10:29-31**

To blaspheme is extremely dangerous. If a Christian does not know better, ignorance is in operation and I do not believe God holds them responsible. On the other hand, if a Christian does know better and takes the position that the things of God are not of God, but are of the devil, that person is in a dangerous position with God Almighty. Judgment for them in making such a statement will depend on the level of their spiritual development when the statement was made.

If you believe that speaking in other tongues is not for you, then at least do not equate this experience with being demon possessed or of the devil.

Objection Two:
Tongues Passed Away

Many believe that tongues passed away after the Bible was completed, and that tongues ceased after the apostles' deaths. Those who believe this objection acknowledge that believers once spoke in other tongues as a sign of supernatural occurrence in the Church while the Bible was being written. Then, once the Scriptures were completed, tongues were supposedly no longer needed.

Actually, there are more people speaking in tongues today than at any time in history. Tongues can be traced from the Day of Pentecost—through to the history of those murdered and martyred for holding fast to speaking in tongues in the Middle East—to those finally gaining the experience in Europe and the United States. For two thousand years, speaking in tongues has been documented and has never died out. The Pentecostal experience was first spoken of by the Old Testament prophet Joel:

> **And it shall come to pass afterward, that I will pour out my spirit upon all flesh; and your sons and your daughters shall prophesy, your old men shall dream dreams, your young men shall see visions: And also upon the servants and upon the handmaids in those days will I pour out my spirit.**
> **Joel 2:28,29**

The assumption that tongues was dependent upon the apostles' life spans or upon the length of time it took the Bible to be written has absolutely no scriptural basis.

The Bible was not assembled as a book until over three hundred years after Jesus Christ was resurrected. If we believe tongues were in operation only until the Bible was completed, then we would have to agree that this manifestation was in existence for at least three hundred years. This would mean God favored the believers who lived in the first three hundred years of the Church more than those of us in the last seventeen hundred years. But the Bible says, **God is no respecter of persons** (Acts 10:34).

Now let's address the assumption that tongues were dependent upon the apostles' longevity. What about people younger than the apostles who were filled with the Holy Ghost with the evidence of speaking in other tongues during their ministry? (Acts 8:14-18; 10:44-46; 19:6,7.) What happened to their ability to speak in tongues after the last apostle died? Was it lost? There is no Scripture to support such a belief.

Acts 2:16 gives a scriptural explanation to the first occurrence of people speaking in other tongues. Actually this entire chapter answers the majority of questions on the subject of tongues. The first occurrence of people being filled with the Holy Ghost caused a great commotion. People were asking, "What is this? What does it mean?" Peter stood up and gave them an answer.

> **But this is that which was spoken by the prophet Joel;**
>
> **And it shall come to pass in the last days, saith God, I will pour out of my Spirit upon all flesh: and your sons and your daughters shall prophesy, and your young men shall see visions, and your old men shall dream dreams.**
>
> **Acts 2:16,17**

Peter explained that what they were hearing — people speaking in other tongues — was exactly what Joel prophesied in the Old Testament. **This is that**, Peter said. Peter continued this sermon in verse 33:

> **Therefore being by the right hand of God exalted, and having received of the Father the promise of the Holy Ghost, he hath shed forth this, which ye now see and hear.**

The Holy Ghost cannot be seen. However, the *result* of one being filled with the Holy Ghost can be seen and heard: people speaking in other tongues.

For the promise is unto you, and to your children, and to all that are afar off, even as many as the Lord our God shall call.

Acts 2:39

For the promise.... What promise? The promise of the Holy Ghost, which has been shed forth and which you now see and hear. This verse assures us that the promise of the Holy Ghost with the evidence of speaking in other tongues is for you, your children, and everyone who receives Jesus as Lord and Savior.

Ponder these questions: Does God still call people? Are you a part of that far off generation mentioned in verse 39? I answer yes to both questions. A yes means that this promise of the Holy Ghost, which they heard and saw two thousand years ago, is still for us today. The promise never died out.

Objection Three:
Only the Apostles Could Minister
the Infilling

Some people maintain that only the apostles could minister the infilling of the Holy Ghost with the evidence of speaking in other tongues. The assumption that speaking in tongues died out with the last apostle's death carries much credence because no one else would seemingly have been able to minister the infilling of the Holy Ghost to those desiring Him. However, Acts 9 deflates this belief.

In the beginning of Chapter 9, Saul was on a journey to arrest Christians. He was saved on the road to Damascus through a supernatural appearance of Jesus Christ. Jesus told Saul to go into the city and there he would be told what to do next. Saul arose and went to the city, but for three days he was blind and did not eat or drink.

And there was a *certain disciple* at Damascus, named Ananias; and to him said the Lord in a vision, Ananias. And he said, Behold, I am here, Lord.

And the Lord said unto him, Arise, and go into the street which is called Straight, and enquire in the house of Judas for one called Saul, of Tarsus: for, behold, he prayeth,

And hath seen in a vision a man named Ananias coming in, and putting his hand on him, that he might receive his sight.

Acts 9:10-12

Ananias was that certain disciple, but that certain disciple could also be you. *Disciple* simply means a follower or student of Jesus Christ. Ananias was not one of the twelve apostles of Jesus. Furthermore, he did not want to deal with Saul, and he gave the Lord his reasons, but the Lord encouraged and assured Ananias that Saul was His chosen vessel.

And Ananias went his way, and entered into the house; and putting his hands on him said, Brother Saul, the Lord, even Jesus, that appeared unto thee in the way as thou camest, hath sent me, that thou mightest receive thy sight, and be filled with the Holy Ghost.

Acts 9:17

From this passage of Scripture in Acts, we can now understand why Paul said, **I thank my God, I speak with tongues more than ye all** (1 Corinthians 14:18). Based on Paul's declaration, we can see that he was thankful for being able to speak in tongues. This champion tongue-talker of the New Testament was ministered the infilling of the Holy Ghost by a certain disciple, Ananias. Therefore, it is unlikely that the apostles were the only ones endowed with the ability to minister the infilling of the Holy Ghost with the evidence of other tongues. There is no scriptural reference to support this objection.

Objection Four:
Tongues Are Not for Everyone

Some believe that tongues are not for everyone, but are for a special, select few. A few scriptures are generally used in an effort to validate this objection.

> **To another the working of miracles; to another prophecy; to another discerning of spirits; to another divers kinds of tongues; to another the interpretation of tongues.**
>
> **1 Corinthians 12:10**

People interpret this verse to mean that not every single believer receives the gift of speaking in tongues. Then in verse 30, Paul is asking rhetorical questions: **Have all the gifts of healing? do all speak with tongues? do all interpret?** Obviously, the answer to each question is no. So, based on this scripture, people say, "See, maybe some people do speak in tongues, but it is not for everyone."

What you should do now is try to understand just exactly what is being discussed in this passage of Scripture. The rule for scriptural interpretation is that all Scripture must be interpreted in light of all other Scripture which deals with the same topic.

First of all then, being filled with the Holy Ghost is not the topic under discussion in these verses. The topic being discussed is spiritual gifts, or gifts of the Spirit. Only two of the nine gifts of the Spirit are unique to the New Testament. The other seven existed in the Old Testament. But all nine gifts, which are in manifestation in the Church age, are taught in this chapter.

Starting in verse 8, the nine gifts (public ministry manifestations) are being discussed: the word of wisdom, the word of knowledge, discerning of spirits, etc. In public ministry, the Spirit divides the gifts severally as He wills. Not everyone is in public ministry. The following verses give the full context of this matter.

> And God hath set some in the church, first apostles, secondarily prophets, thirdly teachers, after that miracles, then gifts of healings, helps, governments, diversities of tongues.
>
> Are all apostles? are all prophets? are all teachers? are all workers of miracles?
>
> Have all the gifts of healing? do all speak with tongues? do all interpret?
>
> But covet earnestly the best gifts: and yet shew I unto you a more excellent way.
>
> **1 Corinthians 12:28-31**

Remember, the topic under discussion here is public ministry. Not every believer is equipped by God to publicly minister in divers kinds of tongues. And not every believer is equipped by God to interpret tongues given in public services. In the same context we can see that not every believer is an apostle or prophet or teacher.

Therefore, being filled with the Holy Ghost with the evidence of speaking in other tongues has absolutely nothing to do with these Scriptures.

It is totally illogical to take a segment of Scripture out of its context and try to apply it to something to which it does not relate. For example, it is ridiculous to read in the Bible, **Judas went out and hung himself,** and say that verse gives you license to go out and hang yourself.

As you read the Bible, you must determine:

1) if Scripture is speaking literally or allegorically;

2) the context of the verse in order to resolve correct meaning; and

3) what other Scripture has to say about the same subject.

In view of these rules, it is obvious that this passage of Scripture does not prove that being filled with the Holy

Ghost with the evidence of speaking in other tongues is not for everyone.

Objection Five:
Tongues Shall Cease

The basis for the objection that tongues shall cease is found in 1 Corinthians 13:8:

> **Charity never faileth: but whether there be prophecies, they shall fail; whether there be tongues, they shall cease; whether there be knowledge, it shall vanish away.**

I agree that tongues will cease. The question is, "When shall tongues cease?" The answer to this question is given in the context of 1 Corinthians 13:10 which states,

> **But when that which is perfect is come, then that which is in part shall be done away.**

Some people think *the perfect* is the Word of God. They believe that upon completion of the Bible's writing, tongues were no longer needed because the perfect had come. But Paul doesn't stop there.

> **When I was a child, I spake as a child, I understood as a child, I thought as a child: but when I became a man, I put away childish things.**
>
> **For now we see through a glass, darkly; but then face to face: now I know in part; but then shall I know even as also I am known.**
> **1 Corinthians 13:11,12**

How will we know when that which is perfect has come? The standard of verse 12 is, **but then face to face.** What is the "face to face" he is referring to? It is when we will see Jesus face to face. Paul continues by saying, **now I know in part; but then shall I know even as also I am known.** Even though the Bible has been completely written, has the perfect come? No! Jesus is not standing face to face with us yet.

Do we know *everything* now? Are all our questions answered? Do we know as much about ourselves as God knows? Since the answer to all three of these questions is no, there must be something that will help us completely understand all things. That something is seeing Jesus face to face. Now we only know part of everything, but then shall we know even as also we are known. Then we will know what Jesus knows. He is known as the perfect and true One. When He comes, we will see Him face to face, and He will make all things known to us. That which is perfect is Jesus. When the perfect comes, we will have no need for tongues.

Let's take a close look at verse 8, which will further address this objection.

Charity never faileth: but whether there be prophecies, they shall fail; whether there be tongues, they shall cease; whether there be knowledge, it shall vanish away.

1 Corinthians 13:8

If we believe that tongues ceased when the Bible was written, we must also believe knowledge ceased when the Bible was written, because both are in the same verse. We cannot take our spiritual knives and cut out certain parts of a verse, leave other parts intact, and build a scripturally sound and correct doctrine. Knowledge certainly has not vanished!

With regard to the validity that knowledge has remained, we can look to the Bible for support. Remember, all Scripture must be interpreted in light of all other Scripture which deals with the same subject. Daniel 12:4 says that in the end **knowledge shall be increased.** Consequently, since knowledge will increase and not vanish, then speaking in other tongues will not cease in the last days either.

The objection that tongues ceased when the Bible was completed cannot be substantiated in light of the Bible's teaching.

Objection Six:
Salvation and Baptism of
the Holy Ghost Are One

Some people maintain that you receive the baptism of the Holy Ghost when you are saved. They contend that there is not a separate experience and that you receive all of the Holy Ghost that it is possible to receive when you accept Jesus as your Lord and Savior.

But there is no Scripture to support this claim. Usually, people who believe this objection have not remained hungry and thirsty for God. They are satisfied with what they have and deny there is something more. Nevertheless, the Bible indicates there is an experience with the Holy Spirit subsequent to and distinct from salvation.

And when he had said this, he breathed on them, and saith unto them, Receive ye the Holy Ghost.
John 20:22

John tells us that Jesus breathed on the disciples after His resurrection. They received the Holy Ghost, were born again, and became new creatures at that moment. Jesus was not confused in the first chapter of Acts when He commanded the apostles to *wait for the promise of the Father*, which He called a baptism in the Holy Ghost.

And, being assembled together with them, commanded them that they should not depart from Jerusalem, but wait for the promise of the Father, which, saith he, ye have heard of me.
For John truly baptized with water; but ye shall be baptized with the Holy Ghost not many days hence.
Acts 1:4,5

Approximately forty-seven days prior to Acts 1:4,5, Jesus had said to the disciples, **Receive ye the Holy Ghost.** He was telling them not to leave until they were baptized with the Holy Ghost. It would appear that Jesus' thinking is messed up, but notice verse 8.

> **But ye shall receive power, after that the Holy Ghost is come upon you: and ye shall be witnesses unto me both in Jerusalem, and in all Judaea, and in Samaria, and unto the uttermost part of the earth.**
>
> **Acts 1:8**

Obviously, when Jesus breathed on them for salvation, they did not receive all the Holy Ghost had to offer them. It is not a question of whether you get *all* the Holy Ghost or not. The Holy Ghost is not two people. However, He does have more than one *function*.

It is true that you receive the indwelling presence of the Holy Ghost when you are saved. But the *indwelling* presence of the Holy Ghost is not synonymous with the *infilling* of the Holy Ghost, which carries with it the evidence of speaking in other tongues. This is exactly what happened to those who obeyed Jesus' command and tarried in Jerusalem to receive the power of the Holy Ghost.

> **And when the day of Pentecost was fully come, they were all with one accord in one place.**
>
> **And suddenly there came a sound from heaven as of a rushing mighty wind, and it filled all the house where they were sitting.**
>
> **And there appeared unto them cloven tongues like as of fire, and it sat upon each of them.**
>
> **And they were all filled with the Holy Ghost, and began to speak with other tongues, as the Spirit gave them utterance.**
>
> **Acts 2:1-4**

If they had already received *all* that was available to them, Jesus would not have instructed them to wait for the promise of the Holy Ghost.

Later on, in Paul's travels to Ephesus, the book of Acts supports this point. Paul asks some disciples:

> **Have ye received the Holy Ghost since ye believed?**
>
> **Acts 19:2**

Whether these people were saved or not when Paul met them was not the question. The spiritual significance of this verse is the question itself. If they had received all there was to the ministry of the Holy Ghost when they believed, why would Paul ask, **Have ye received the Holy Ghost** *since* **ye believed?** There is obviously something more.

Earlier in the book of John, Jesus referred to the infilling of the Holy Spirit:

> **In the last day, that great day of the feast, Jesus stood and cried, saying, If any man thirst, let him come unto me, and drink.**
>
> **He that believeth on me, as the scripture hath said, out of his belly shall flow rivers of living water.**
>
> **John 7:37,38**

The distinctions between the *indwelling* presence of the Holy Spirit received at the moment of salvation and the *infilling* of the Holy Spirit (also called *the baptism of the Holy Spirit*) accompanied by speaking in other tongues, are supported by numerous scriptural examples.

Objection Seven: Spirit-filled With No Evidence of Speaking in Tongues

Some believers argue, "I am filled with the Holy Ghost and I do not speak in other tongues. I don't care what anybody says, I know I am filled with the Holy Ghost." If you identify with this objection, consider 2 Timothy 3:16 which says, **All scripture is given by inspiration of God, and is profitable for doctrine, for reproof, for correction, for instruction in righteousness.** With this Scripture fresh in mind, let's look again to the book of Acts.

> **And they were all filled with the Holy Ghost, and began to speak with other tongues, as the Spirit gave them utterance.**
>
> **Acts 2:4**

While Peter yet spake these words, the Holy Ghost fell on all them which heard the word.

And they of the circumcision which believed were astonished, as many as came with Peter, because that on the Gentiles also was poured out the gift of the Holy Ghost.

For they heard them speak with tongues, and magnify God. Then answered Peter,

Can any man forbid water, that these should not be baptized, which have received the Holy Ghost as well as we?

Acts 10:44-47

And when Paul had laid his hands upon them, the Holy Ghost came on them; and they spake with tongues, and prophesied.

Acts 19:6

There are five recorded instances in the Bible of people being filled with the Holy Ghost. In each of these cases, the way that people knew they were filled with the Holy Ghost was the evidence of speaking in other tongues.

As we will look at more fully in Chapter 2, in the three passages cited above, tongues literally manifested in all involved. In a fourth instance, when Peter and John prayed for Philip's Samarian converts (Acts 8:14-24), there is no mention of tongues. But there was an obvious sign to Simon the sorcerer when he **saw that through laying on of the apostles' hands the Holy Ghost was given, he offered them money** (v. 18). Simon offered Peter and John money to buy the Holy Ghost's gift. And Paul says in 1 Corinthians 14:22 that tongues are a sign to unbelievers. So for Simon to have *seen* that the Holy Ghost was given, there must have been a sign: something visible and/or audible in the physical realm.

Finally, Paul's baptism of the Holy Ghost experience, making up the fifth example in Scripture, does not show him speaking in tongues when ministered to by Ananias in

Acts 9. But in 1 Corinthians 14:18 he gives testimony to the fact that, **I thank God I speak with tongues more than ye all** (v.18), and this within the most powerful teaching in Scripture given in reference to God's will for tongues in the Church.

Today, some believers claim to be filled with the Holy Ghost without the evidence of tongues. It is impossible. Tongues have always been the *initial evidence* of receiving the infilling or baptism of the Holy Ghost.

Paul teaches us in 2 Corinthians 13:1, **In the mouth of two or three witnesses shall every word be established.** On the issue of tongues, the Bible did not give two or three witnesses, but *five!*

Objection Eight:
Jesus Didn't Speak in Tongues

Some people rationalize, "Since Jesus didn't speak in other tongues, why should we?" Jesus did not speak in other tongues, because He ministered under the Old Testament. Tongues and interpretation of tongues did not exist until after His ascension. Speaking in tongues occurred for the first time on the Day of Pentecost:

> **And when the day of Pentecost was fully come, they were all with one accord in one place.**
>
> **And suddenly there came a sound from heaven as of a rushing mighty wind, and it filled all the house where they were sitting.**
>
> **And there appeared unto them cloven tongues like as of fire, and it sat upon each of them.**
>
> **And they were all filled with the Holy Ghost, and began to speak with other tongues, as the Spirit gave them utterance.**
>
> **Acts 2:1-4**

Jesus ministered as an Old Testament prophet, although He was in the transitional period before the new covenant was established. Elijah did not speak in tongues. Moses did not speak in tongues. King David did not speak in tongues. Therefore, Jesus did not speak in tongues either. They could not, because *it was not available under the Old Testament covenant.* The Holy Ghost, the Comforter, had not been given nor could He be given until Jesus paid the price for sin on the cross, was resurrected, and ascended to the Father.

Seven gifts were in operation in the Old Testament, but on the Day of Pentecost, the seven gifts were expanded to nine — tongues and the interpretation of tongues were added. These two additional gifts are the supernatural mark of the Church age (Mark 16:17), a sign to the unbeliever (1 Corinthians 14:22), used to edify the Church (1 Corinthians 14:4,5) and to intercede to our Heavenly Father (Romans 8:26).

The New Testament brought with it tongues and the interpretation of tongues. By the time the Holy Ghost came and tongues were manifested, Jesus was with the Father in heaven. He had done all that was necessary to save us and give us both the *indwelling presence* and *infilling power* of the Holy Ghost.

I trust the answers to these eight common objections to the infilling of the Holy Ghost with the evidence of speaking in other tongues will be a helpful resource for you.

Chapter Two
Bible Evidence to Receiving the Infilling of the Holy Ghost

By the time you complete this study, there should be no doubt in your mind of the reality of the infilling of the Holy Ghost, and that it is subsequent to and separate from salvation. You will also be able to share these rich scriptural truths with others.

I have noticed through the years in helping hundreds of believers receive the infilling of the Holy Ghost, that after they have received, they know it is true, but still have difficulty proving *how* and *why*. They know a little about it from the Bible, but they can't systematically open up the Bible and go through the Scriptures with others. Therefore, I believe there is a legitimate need for this type of teaching.

In the gospel of John as Jesus was ministering to the woman at the well, He introduces water as an analogical comparison to the Holy Ghost.

Jesus answered and said unto her, Whosoever drinketh of this water shall thirst again:

But whosoever drinketh of the water that I shall give him shall never thirst; but the water that I shall give him shall be in him a well of water springing up into everlasting life.

John 4:13,14

In Scripture, water, wine, oil and fire are all types of the Holy Ghost. Jesus is talking about water coming from a well. Isaiah 12:3 says, **Therefore with joy shall ye draw water out of the wells of salvation.**

In John's gopel, Jesus is telling the woman that if she drinks this natural water, she will be thirsty again, but once she drinks of the well of salvation she will never thirst again. Eternal life will be imparted into her spirit. From that well of salvation it will spring up in her and she will be aware of everlasting life.

Later on in the gospel of John, the Holy Spirit was described by Jesus as *rivers of living water.*

> **In the last day, that great day of the feast, Jesus stood and cried, saying, If any man thirst, let him come unto me, and drink.**
>
> **He that believeth on me, as the scripture hath said, out of his belly shall flow *rivers of living water.***
>
> **(But this spake he of the Spirit, which they that believe on him should receive: for the Holy Ghost was not yet given; because that Jesus was not yet glorified.)**
> **John 7:37-39**

Instead of referring to a well of water, Jesus makes reference to rivers of living water. There is a big difference between a well of water and a flowing river. You draw life from a well for the nourishment of your body, but a river releases power. A river flows, as in a stream.

Another forceful energy is fire. As a young boy, I was fascinated with fire. Even after I was born again, I was still fascinated by fire. We would get our fireplace going and I would just sit there watching the flames, the embers and the ashes, enjoying the warmth.

One day I was meditating on the thought that there is nothing so consuming and powerful as fire. I mean, fire rages! Recently, we saw a news clip from California where the winds whipped up a fire in the woods, and thousands of acres of timberland and brush were at its mercy. Fire will rampage through anything flammable. When it isn't stopped, it consumes everything in its path.

As I watched this fire, the Scripture came to me about the river of water of life in heaven. Suddenly, it dawned on me that there is something more powerful, more consuming than fire, and that is water. Have you ever visited or seen pictures of the great Hoover Dam? If the Hoover Dam could have been broken open to spill out its water on the California fire, the flames would have gone out immediately. That water would have overwhelmed and suffocated it.

Water, rivers of water and raging torrents of river water denote *immense* power! The rivers of living water Jesus spoke of in John 7 are speaking of power — a spiritual power that can flow from every believer.

In John 7 Jesus said the Holy Ghost was not yet given because He was not yet glorified. In John 20 we find Him reunited with His disciples after He was glorified.

> **Then the same day at evening, being the first day of the week, when the doors were shut where the disciples were assembled for fear of the Jews, came Jesus and stood in the midst, and saith unto them, Peace be unto you.**
>
> **And when he had so said, He shewed unto them his hands and his side. Then were the disciples glad, when they saw the Lord.**
>
> **Then said Jesus to them again, Peace be unto you: as my Father hath sent me, even so send I you.**
>
> **And when he had said this, he breathed on them, and saith unto them, Receive ye the Holy Ghost.**
> **John 20:19-22**

Say this out loud: *"Jesus breathed on them and said, Receive ye the Holy Ghost."*

Do you believe that when Jesus breathed on them and said, **Receive ye the Holy Ghost**, that they received the Holy Ghost? This bears noticeable resemblance to the creation of man in the book of Genesis.

> **And the Lord God formed man of the dust of the ground, and breathed into his nostrils the breath of life; and man became a living soul.**
>
> **Genesis 2:7**

In the very beginning, when God created man, He breathed into him the breath of life. Then, in John 20 when Jesus recreated man's spirit, **he breathed on them, and saith unto them, Receive ye the Holy Ghost.**

When the Holy Ghost comes inside of you, you are recreated. You are made a new creation in Christ Jesus (2 Corinthians 5:17). Eternal life is imparted into your spirit. Jesus said, **Receive ye the Holy Ghost,** and these men were born again. We could say they received the *indwelling presence* of the Holy Ghost when Jesus breathed His Spirit into them.

Now, I want to show you a very *common* passage of Scripture to Pentecostal, full gospel believers. Jesus is still talking to the same people we were reading about in John 20. He has just breathed on them and said, **Receive ye the Holy Ghost.** He is talking to born-again believers. What else did He say to them?

> **And he said unto them, Go ye into all the world, and preach the gospel to every creature.**
>
> **He that believeth and is baptized shall be saved; but he that believeth not shall be damned.**
>
> **Mark 16:15,16**

Notice, Jesus is talking about salvation in verse 16.

> **He that believeth and is baptized shall be saved.**

But let's keep reading.

> **And these signs shall follow them that believe; In my name shall they cast out devils; they shall speak with new tongues.**
>
> **Mark 16:17**

Jesus has suddenly switched from salvation to talking about signs that would characterize the believing ones. See how this is separate and distinct. In verse 15 you believed, were baptized and born again. Then He changes gears. He talks about signs that follow the believer — casting out devils, speaking with new tongues and taking up serpents. If they drink any deadly thing, it shall not hurt them. They will lay hands on the sick, and the sick shall recover.

There are five signs that should follow every believer. One of these signs is speaking in tongues.

When Jesus shared *The Great Commission* with these men, they didn't have a clue as to what He was saying. Jesus often said things that took a while for His disciples to understand. Jesus said, **I have yet many things to say unto you, but ye cannot bear them now** (John 16:12).

He told these born-again believers, these people whom He breathed on, that now they were commissioned to go and take this message and share it; that everyone who believes and is baptized will be saved. Then, once they are saved, five signs will follow the believing ones. One of these five signs is that they will speak with other tongues.

Luke, an apostle and the author of the book of Acts, documents some events of Jesus that are very important for us to understand. Acts 1:4 records the moments before Jesus' departure from earth, after which He was to be seated at the right hand of the Father until He comes again. Before He left Jesus shared some final instructions.

> **And, being assembled together with them, commanded them that they should not depart from Jerusalem, but wait for the promise of the Father, which, saith he, ye have heard of me.**
>
> **For John truly baptized with water; but ye shall be baptized with the Holy Ghost not many days hence.**
>
> **Acts 1:4,5**

Now, as you look at verse 8, you will notice what seems to be a slightly different perspective.

> **But ye shall receive power, after that the Holy Ghost is come upon you: and ye shall be witnesses unto me both in Jerusalem, and in all Judaea, and in Samaria, and unto the uttermost part of the earth.**

We established in John 20 that these people were born again, because Jesus breathed on them and said, **Receive ye the Holy Ghost.** Conversely, in Acts 1:8, He says that **ye shall receive power, after that the Holy Ghost is come upon you.** Is Jesus confused, or is Church tradition confused? In one instance, the Holy Ghost is received and later Jesus says they will receive power after the Holy Ghost has come upon them.

Notice the phrase, **the Holy Ghost is come upon you.** The Spirit comes *in* you when you are born again. Now He is talking about the Spirit coming *upon* you. In verse 4 He talked about the **promise of the Father.** He mentioned that they heard this about Him from John the Baptist. When John was baptizing with water, he said, **I indeed baptize you with water; but one mightier than I cometh, the latchet of whose shoes I am not worthy to unloose: he shall baptize you with the Holy Ghost and with fire** (Luke 3:16).

An interesting characteristic about God is that when He wants you to get something, He repeats it. Any time you see something repeated in two of four gospels, it is important. When it is in three of the four gospels, it is real important. When it is in all four gospels, which is rare, you can't miss it!

In four out of four gospels, John the Baptist said that Jesus will baptize us in the Holy Ghost (Matthew 3:11, Mark 1:8, Luke 3:16, and John 1:33). This is a message from heaven God wanted us to receive.

In Acts 1:4 Jesus *commanded* His followers to wait for the promise of the Father — the Holy Spirit. He did not suggest nor did He merely infer. He didn't say, "If you want a blessing, hang around." He didn't say, "I've got a good idea." He didn't say, "I want to give you some advice that will better you in your Christian walk." The Bible says that when He had gathered the apostles together, He gave a command. What does *command* mean? It means, demand. Jesus demanded that they not leave Jerusalem until they received the **promise of the Father.**

Old time Pentecostals believed in *tarrying*. They read this verse and came up with the idea of tarrying to receive the Holy Ghost. Of course, if you are going to take this verse literally, you would have to tarry in *Jerusalem*. That's not the case at all. Even though they had been born again, Jesus demanded that they not leave Jerusalem until the Spirit of God came upon them and they were endued with power from on high.

If it was that important for Jesus to make it a command, what right do we have today to determine this experience is not for us? What right do we have to say this experience passed away, that it is not for us, that it is just for some people, or that it is of the devil?

Let's do a systematic, step-by-step study of this experience from the Bible. It doesn't matter what your Aunt Martha or Grandma Millie thought about it. We need to know what the Bible has to say on the subject.

In Mark 16 Jesus told the disciples, **Go ye into all the world, and preach the gospel to every creature. He that believeth and is baptized shall be saved** (vv. 15,16). Certainly, these eleven disciples must have immediately started preaching after they were given the commission, because by the time we read Acts 1:15, their number had grown to 120. Those 120 believers **were all filled with the Holy Ghost** in Acts 2:4.

I remember talking to a Catholic lady who wanted to get filled with the Holy Ghost. Some people say, "Oh, you can't get a Catholic filled with the Holy Ghost. They're not even saved." Many *religious* people think that! I had been teaching on the infilling experience, and this dear Catholic lady said, "I don't know about this, but I think from what you have said, I want to receive this experience."

So I opened up the Bible to Acts 1:14 and said, "Did you know Mary, the mother of Jesus, spoke in tongues?" Mary, the mother of Jesus, received the infilling of the Holy Ghost in Acts 2, because she was one of the 120 waiting in the Upper Room. That dear little lady received instantly.

Here's the account of the Day of Pentecost when Jesus' family and friends were assembled in the Upper Room. These 120 people were now Christians, born again, and they had gathered together to wait as Jesus had commanded.

> **And when the day of Pentecost was fully come, they were all with one accord in one place.**
>
> **And suddenly there came a sound from heaven as of a rushing mighty wind, and it filled all the house where they were sitting.**
>
> **And there appeared unto them cloven tongues like as of fire, and it sat upon each of them.**
>
> **And they were all filled with the Holy Ghost, and began to speak with other tongues, as the Spirit gave them utterance.**
>
> **Acts 2:1-4**

You may ask, "I thought they already had the Holy Ghost?" In fact, they did! They were born again, but in this instance they were receiving an additional experience with the Holy Ghost. They were **filled with the Holy Ghost, and began to speak with other tongues, as the Spirit gave them utterance.** They went out from the Upper Room staggering under the power of God. The

Bible actually says that those who saw them thought they were drunk.

I want you to notice something before we go any further in our study. I want you to be aware of the reaction the religious people had to this experience, because religious people from all over the world were gathered in Jerusalem for the Feast of Pentecost.

> **And they were all amazed, and were in doubt, saying one to another, What meaneth this?**
>
> **Others mocking said, These men are full of new wine.**
>
> Acts 2:12,13

They were amazed! They were in doubt and they were mocking. Two thousand years later *religious* people still get amazed and doubt, and mock this experience. Peter then got up and said, **For these are not drunken, as ye suppose** (v. 15). Then in verse 16 Peter goes on to quote the prophecy, **This is that which was spoken by the prophet Joel.**

You can divide the religious community up into these same two categories to this very day. There is one division that doubts in amazement and mockingly says, "What meaneth this?" Then, there is another that says, "This is that." **This is that** computes to the *promise of the Father!* Now observe verses 17 and 18.

> **And it shall come to pass in the last days, saith God, I will pour out of my Spirit upon all flesh: and your sons and your daughters shall prophesy, and your young men shall see visions, and your old men shall dream dreams:**
>
> **And on my servants and on my handmaidens I will pour out in those days of my Spirit; and they shall prophesy.**
>
> Acts 2:17,18

Aren't you glad God is no respecter of persons?

Peter went on to explain what happened after quoting Joel and finished by preaching his first sermon.

Therefore being by the right of hand of God exalted, and having received of the Father the promise of the Holy Ghost, he hath shed forth this, which you now see and hear.

Acts 2:33

Luke records that Jesus told His followers to tarry in Jerusalem until they were endued with power from on high. Observe how Luke phrases what Jesus said.

And, behold, I send the promise of my Father upon you: but tarry ye in the city of Jerusalem, until ye be endued with power from on high.

Luke 24:49

This is important because Jesus called this enduement **the promise of my Father.** Peter is also saying that this is the promise of the Holy Ghost which Jesus told us about. And, as he experienced, you can see it and hear it. This is interesting because when someone gets born again, you don't really see anything happen outwardly. At least, you don't see what happens on the inside. If they whisper their confession, you can't even hear them. You could be sitting on the back row; you could see someone answer an altar call, but you don't really know what happened. You don't see it and you may not hear the moment they accept Jesus Christ.

In Acts 2 the believers were staggering around because of the infilling of the Holy Ghost and spoke in other tongues. Their experience could be seen and heard. The entire second chapter of Acts talks about them speaking in many different languages. As the multitude hears and sees, they want to know how to get saved; they are convinced that this is of God.

Then Peter said unto them, Repent, and be baptized every one of you in the name of Jesus Christ for the

remission of sins, and ye shall receive the gift of the Holy Ghost.

Acts 2:38

Now, doesn't this go back to where we started in Mark 16? **He that believeth and is baptized shall be saved.** What did Peter just say to these people? **Repent, and be baptized every one of you in the name of Jesus Christ for the remission of sins.** Doesn't this mean you are saved? If you repent, you are baptized and you believe in the name of Jesus, your sins are washed away and you are born again, aren't you? But He didn't quit there. Notice the word *and*. **And ye shall receive the gift of the Holy Ghost.**

When I was born again in a denominational church, they always said that this verse was talking only about salvation. It is talking about *more* than just salvation. Salvation is never called "the gift of the Holy Ghost." It is called a gift of grace or the gift of salvation. The gift of the Holy Ghost is always used in reference to the infilling of the Holy Spirit.

For the promise is unto you, and to your children, and to all that are afar off, even as many as the Lord our God shall call.

Acts 2:39

What promise? The promise in verse 39 is the identical promise of the Holy Ghost that we read about in verse 33. It is the exact promise that was revealed in Acts chapter 1, verse 4, when Jesus said to **wait for the promise of the Father.** This same promise was seen and heard by witnesses on the Day of Pentecost.

This answers the age-old question, "Did tongues die out when the Bible was finished?" Scripture says this promise is available to everyone who is born again. As long as people keep getting called to repentance and called to salvation, then this experience is available for them. It goes on and on. This promise is available for you and me today.

I want you to look again at Acts 2:1-4. We are going to look at the manifestations of this promise of the Father. The first manifestation was a *sound*. They heard a sound from heaven that was **as of a rushing mighty wind.** Secondly, fire appeared. The *King James Bible* says, **cloven tongues like as of fire.** Literally, it was light. The light of God shone on them. (All through the Old and New Testaments when there was bright shining light, it was oftentimes referred to as fire.) The third demonstration was that they were *heard* speaking in tongues. Fourthly, they acted like drunk people: **These men are full of new wine** (v. 13). These four indications from the Word of God reveal that experiencing the promise of the Father could be seen and heard.

Five Recorded Instances in Acts of the Holy Ghost Baptism

In Acts there are five recorded instances of believers receiving the baptism of the Holy Ghost, or the, infilling, of the Holy Ghost. (Both phrases describe the same experience.) We can learn from these five examples.

FIRST OCCURRENCE

Chapter 8 of Acts takes place some eight years after Acts 2:4, which was the first occurrence of the outpouring of the Holy Spirit and documents the second instance of believers receiving this experience.

SECOND OCCURRENCE

Then Philip went down to the city of Samaria, and preached Christ unto them.

And the people with one accord gave heed unto those things which Philip spake, hearing and seeing the miracles which he did.

For unclean spirits, crying with loud voice, came out of many that were possessed with them: and many taken with palsies, and that were lame, were healed.

> **And there was great joy in that city...**
>
> **But when they believed Philip preaching the things concerning the kingdom of God, and the name of Jesus Christ, they were baptized, both men and women.**
> **Acts 8:5-8,12**

Philip was having a revival, wasn't he? Notice what the Bible says:

1) They gave heed to what he was saying.

2) They believed the things that he preached about the Kingdom.

3) They believed in Jesus.

4) They were baptized.

Now, I want to ask you a question. Were they saved? In Mark 16 Jesus said that those who believe and are baptized shall be saved. Acts 8:12 says they believed Philip preaching the things concerning the Kingdom of God and the name of Jesus, then both men and women were baptized. Were they saved? Of course they were! They received the indwelling presence of the Holy Ghost. They were re-created. They were born again, new creatures in Christ. They were saved!

> **Now when the apostles which were at Jerusalem heard that Samaria had received the word of God, they sent unto them Peter and John:**
>
> **Who, when they were come down, prayed for them, that they might receive the Holy Ghost:**
>
> **(For as yet he was fallen upon none of them: only they were baptized in the name of the Lord Jesus.)**
> **Acts 8:14-16**

They were born again and indwelt by the Spirit of God. The apostles in Jerusalem had heard about it. So they sent in the two specialists, Peter and John, because the Holy Ghost had not yet fallen on these people. The Samaritans were born again, they believed in Jesus and they were baptized, but they weren't speaking in other tongues. They hadn't experienced any of the manifestations that we read about in the second chapter of Acts.

The baptism of the Holy Ghost is a subsequent experience to salvation. It is distinct from your born-again experience. This is evidenced by the fact that the apostles in Jerusalem heard about it and sent Peter and John to minister this experience to them. Let's see what happens next!

> **Then laid they their hands on them, and they received the Holy Ghost.**
>
> **And *when Simon saw* that through laying on of the apostles' hands the Holy Ghost was given, he offered them money,**
>
> **Saying, Give me also this power, that on whomsoever I lay hands, he may receive the Holy Ghost.**
>
> **But Peter said unto him, Thy money perish with thee, because thou hast thought that the gift of God may be purchased with money.**
>
> **Thou hast neither part nor lot in this *matter:* for thy heart is not right in the sight of God.**
>
> **Acts 8:17-21**

You may be thinking, "It doesn't say anything at all about manifestations in this chapter." Oh, yes it does. First of all, let's look at verse 18 **when Simon saw....** What did Acts 2:33 say? **Having received of the Father the promise of the Holy Ghost, he hath shed forth this, which ye now see and hear.** Simon saw that through the laying on of the apostles' hands the Holy Ghost was given. He saw them doing something didn't he?

The second proof is verse 21 of Acts chapter 8 when Peter reprimands Simon, saying, **Thou hast neither part nor lot in this matter.** The word *matter* in the Greek is the same root word that is translated *utterance* in Acts 2:4. In essence, Peter said that Simon had neither part nor lot in this utterance. What utterance is Peter talking about? Could it be the utterances that were heard in Acts 2:4 — the supernatural manifestation of tongues as the Spirit gave utterance?

What was this uttering that Simon *heard*? What was this manifestation that Simon *saw*? Simon was willing to pay money for what he saw and heard, but Peter said that he couldn't buy it, because the promise of the Father is the *gift* of the Holy Ghost. This gift is given to those whose hearts are right in the sight of God, and obviously Simon's heart was not right.

Can you see that the examples of utterances are the same in Acts 2:4 and Acts 8:17-21? Do you recognize the similarities in the experience and the manifestations?

THIRD OCCURRENCE

> And as he journeyed, he came near Damascus: and suddenly there shined round about him a light from heaven:
>
> And he fell to the earth, and heard a voice saying unto him, Saul, Saul, why persecutest thou me?
>
> And he said, Who art thou, Lord? And the Lord said, I am Jesus whom thou persecutest: it is hard for thee to kick against the pricks.
>
> And he trembling and astonished said, Lord, what wilt thou have me to do? And the Lord said unto him, Arise, and go into the city, and it shall be told thee what thou must do.
>
> And the men which journeyed with him stood speechless, hearing a voice, but seeing no man.
>
> **Acts 9:3-7**

Previously, in this same chapter, Saul is breathing out threatenings and trying to slaughter the disciples. By the time we get to verse 5, he is calling Jesus, "Lord." Why is he calling Him *Lord*? He is even following Jesus' directions.

Jesus is telling Saul to go to Damascus and wait there for instructions. Saul is obedient to wait three days and three nights for the Lord to talk to him.

I am confident that Saul was born again right there on that road to Damascus. Don't tell me you wouldn't get born again if you were driving down the highway, a bright light knocked you out of your car and a voice from that light began talking to you! After you said, "Who are you?" and He answered, "I am Jesus," you would say something like, "Yes, sir, whatever You say I will do."

In Acts 9:15 when Jesus speaks with Ananias, He calls Saul **a chosen vessel unto me**. Saul's heart was changed. Jesus told him that he was pushing against the conviction that He had been giving him. He straightened up in a hurry. Now he is **a chosen vessel**. Ananias refers to him as "Brother Saul." If he was unsaved, he sure wouldn't call him *brother*. (You wouldn't walk up to Adolf Hitler or Ayatollah Khomeini and say, "Brother Khomeini" or "Brother Hitler"!) No, you wouldn't call someone else *brother* or *sister* unless they were Christians.

Therefore, we have three witnesses from the Word of God that Saul is born again prior to his meeting with Ananias.

1) Saul called Jesus "Lord" and did what Jesus told him to do.

2) Jesus called Saul a chosen vessel.

3) Ananias called Saul "brother."

Now we find out what happened when Saul and Ananias meet.

> **And Ananias went his way, and entered into the house; and putting his hands on him said, Brother Saul, the Lord, even Jesus, that appeared unto thee in the way as thou camest, hath sent me, that thou mightest receive thy sight, and be filled with the Holy Ghost.**
>
> **Acts 9:17**

This is interesting, because Jesus didn't tell Ananias to lay hands on Saul for the baptism of the Holy Ghost. Jesus told Ananias to lay hands on Saul so that his eyes would be opened. Ananias was a well-taught believer. It seems as though he reasoned, "As long as we are here, I might as well get you filled with the Holy Ghost, too." After the vision he could have felt an urging from the Lord that he should pray this additional way for Saul. Notice, Saul is born again, but he is being prayed for after his salvation to be filled with the Holy Ghost. This experience is obviously subsequent to and distinct from salvation.

The result of laying on of hands and prayer is instantaneous.

> **And immediately there fell from his eyes as it had been scales: and he received sight forthwith, and arose, and was baptized.**
>
> **Acts 9:18**

Someone is always quick to say, "Yeah, but it doesn't say that he spoke in tongues." It is interesting that people bring this up because in 1 Corinthians 14:18 Paul said, **I thank my God, I speak with tongues more than ye all.** To that whole tongue-talking, wild, fired-up bunch in Corinth, Paul is saying that he speaks in tongues more than all of them. In 1 Corinthians 14:15 Paul admonishes, **I will pray with the spirit, and I will pray with the understanding also: I will sing with the spirit, and I will sing with the understanding also.**

This instance in Acts 9 also answers another question. Some people have the misconception that the Holy Ghost was only administered by the apostles. But did you notice that Ananias was not an apostle? He was what we would call a lay person, a church member, or a disciple of Jesus. He went to Saul, laid hands on him and got him filled with the Holy Ghost. Paul later proclaims that he speaks in tongues more than others in Corinth. Ananias did a good job!

We know for a fact from Scripture, with the possible exception of one or two books, that the entire New Testament was written by tongue talkers. Paul alone, who says he speaks in tongues more than that whole Corinthian church, wrote two-thirds of the New Testament.

FOURTH OCCURRENCE

Acts 10 is the fourth experience listed in the Bible. Notice that every time there has been an experience subsequent to salvation, the evidence manifested is that they spoke in tongues. Now let's look at Peter's preaching in Acts 10.

> **How God anointed Jesus of Nazareth with the Holy Ghost and with power: who went about doing good, and healing all that were oppressed of the devil; for God was with him.**
>
> **And we are witnesses of all things which he did both in the land of the Jews, and in Jerusalem; whom they slew and hanged on a tree:**
>
> **Him God raised up the third day, and shewed him openly;**
>
> **Not to all the people, but unto witnesses chosen before of God, even to us, who did eat and drink with him after he rose from the dead.**
>
> **And he commanded us to preach unto the people, and to testify that it is he which was ordained of God to be the Judge of quick and dead.**
>
> **To him give all the prophets witness, that through his name whosoever believeth in him shall receive remission of sins.**
>
> **Acts 10:38-43**

Can you see that Peter just preached the salvation message of the Gospel? He didn't bother giving an altar call, but somewhere in that salvation message Cornelius got saved. He just listened and made the adjustment in his heart. How do we know that? Look at the next verse: **While**

Peter yet spake these words, the Holy Ghost fell on all them which heard the word.

Notice something else. This event happened ten years after the Day of Pentecost. While Peter was still preaching the Word, the Holy Ghost fell on all them who heard the Word. Then, **they of the circumcision which believed were astonished, as many as came with Peter, because that on the Gentiles also was poured out the gift of the Holy Ghost** (v. 45).

How did those who came with Peter know that these Gentiles received the baptism of the Holy Ghost?

For they heard them speak with tongues, and magnify God. Then answered Peter,

Can any man forbid water, that these should not be baptized, which have received the Holy Ghost as well as we?

And he commanded them to be baptized in the name of the Lord. Then prayed they him to tarry certain days.

Acts 10:46-48

How did Peter know these folks were, in effect, saved by his message? What convinced him that it was okay to baptize these people? Remember, these were Gentiles. These were the first non-Jewish believers listed in the Bible. He has preached the Gospel where Jesus said *whosoever* will believe and is baptized will be saved. How did he know that it is safe to baptize these people? How did he know they had really accepted Jesus as Savior? Because it says in verse 46 that he *heard them speak in tongues.*

Not only did they get saved, they were filled with Holy Ghost! In fact, Peter said they received the same gift he had received! **Can any man forbid water,** Peter asked the witnesses that he had brought with him. What convinced them? **They heard them speak with tongues, and magnify**

God (v. 46). That was the evidence! So they baptized them in water.

Then when Peter and the brethren went back to Jerusalem, they were questioned by the Jerusalem church brethren, "What were you doing down there with those Gentiles, those unclean people?" they asked. So Peter started telling them about the vision and the voice that told him to go and fear no man. Giving his defense, the apostle related how he brought witnesses with him and went to the Gentiles.

> **And the spirit bade me go with them, nothing doubting. Moreover these six brethren accompanied me, and we entered into the man's house:**
>
> **And he shewed us how he had seen an angel in his house, which stood and said unto him, Send men to Joppa, and call for Simon, whose surname is Peter;**
>
> **Who shall tell thee words, whereby thou and all thy house shall be saved.**
>
> **And as I began to speak, the Holy Ghost fell on them, as on us at the beginning.**
>
> **Then remembered I the word of the Lord, how that he said, John indeed baptized with water; but ye shall be baptized with the Holy Ghost.**
>
> **Forasmuch then as God gave them the like gift as he did unto us, who believed on the Lord Jesus Christ; what was I, that I could withstand God?**
>
> **When they heard these things, they held their peace, and glorified God, saying, Then hath God also to the Gentiles granted repentance unto life.**
>
> **Acts 11:12-18**

In Acts 10:45, it says that all who came with Peter were astonished. Peter knew the Gentiles received the same gift that he had received ten years earlier, because he heard the Gentiles speak in tongues. It was this very evidence which convinced Peter that these people were genuinely saved.

He used it in defending himself when he said, **What was I, that I could withstand God.** Peter said, **The Holy Ghost fell on them, as on us at the beginning.** He then went on to say that he remembered what Jesus had said about it ten years earlier.

Then, these members of the church in Jerusalem said, **Then hath God also to the Gentiles granted repentance unto life.** The evidence that convinced the apostles that it was God was the Gentiles' ability to speak in other tongues.

It is startling today that some people say speaking in other tongues is *of the devil.* The early Church said when you speak in tongues, God is alive in your life!

FIFTH OCCURRENCE

Ten years had passed since Peter was at Cornelius' house. It was approximately twenty years after Acts 2:4, and Paul was ministering in Ephesus.

> **And it came to pass, that, while Apollos was at Corinth, Paul having passed through the upper coasts came to Ephesus: and finding certain disciples,**
>
> **He said unto them, Have ye received the Holy Ghost since ye believed? And they said unto him, We have not so much as heard whether there be any Holy Ghost.**
>
> **And he said unto them, Unto what then were ye baptized? And they said, Unto John's baptism.**
>
> **Then said Paul, John verily baptized with the baptism of repentance, saying unto the people, that they should believe on him which should come after him, that is, on Christ Jesus.**
>
> **When they heard this, they were baptized in the name of the Lord Jesus.**
>
> **Acts 19:1-5**

In Mark 16:16 Jesus said, **He that believeth and is baptized shall be saved.** So if you believe and you are baptized, you are saved! These certain disciples were saved when Paul met them then, weren't they? No. They had only received John's baptism of repentence. They were saved in verse 5 after Paul told them of Jesus Christ. Now read verse 6: **And when Paul had laid his hands upon them, the Holy Ghost came on them; and they spake with tongues, and prophesied.**

This verse also confirms that there is an experience with the Holy Ghost subsequent to and distinct from salvation, which is the indwelling, re-creative power of the Holy Ghost.

If we receive all there is of the ministry of the Holy Ghost at the moment of salvation, then the disciples would have spoken in tongues when Jesus breathed on them and said, **Receive ye the Holy Ghost** (John 20:22).

Similarly, the believers in Samaria would have spoken in tongues as soon as they believed and were baptized in the name of Jesus when Philip preached to them in Acts 8:12. They wouldn't have needed the services of the other disciples to minister to them (Acts 8:14-17). So the infilling of the Holy Spirit is a separate and distinct experience.

When Paul asked the Ephesian disciples, **Have ye received the Holy Ghost since ye believed?** he implied that you don't receive all there is concerning the Holy Ghost at the moment of salvation. Of course this does not mean you can't be born again and filled with the Holy Ghost simultaneously like Cornelius and his household did. It simply means that Paul had no witness of this happening in Ephesus.

Notice how the manifestation of the Holy Ghost remains constant. Acts 19:6 says, **And when Paul had laid his hands upon them, the Holy Ghost came on them; and they spake with tongues, and prophesied.**

Five out of five times when people were filled with the Holy Spirit, there were manifestations: sounds, fires, and prophesies. They magnified God, praised Him, and there were tongues. Only one of these manifestations was uniquely present on each occasion. The sign was the evidence of speaking in other tongues! Five times in the Bible believers received the Holy Ghost, and five times they spoke with other tongues. Sometimes there were other signs involved, but the evidence of speaking in other tongues was the consistent indication that believers were filled with the Holy Ghost.

Someone might say, "I believe I was baptized in the Holy Ghost, but I have never spoken in tongues." Then, you are not in line with the Bible. I *didn't* say you did not receive the Holy Ghost. You received the Holy Ghost when you were born again, but you have not received the subsequent experience of the infilling of the Holy Spirit. When you receive this gift from God, you will speak in other tongues. If you have not spoken in other tongues, you have not received this experience. It is the desire and command of Jesus for all of His followers to receive the Holy Ghost. The constant biblical proof of having received is *the ability to speak in other tongues.*

The benefits of this experience are many. Why should you speak in tongues? First, Jesus commanded it (Acts 1:4). He also said in Acts 1:8 that we would be endued with power from on high. So all believers should be interested in supernatural power to be effective witnesses for Jesus Christ. Let's look at a few other verses to see some of the advantages of this experience.

> **For he that speaketh in an unknown tongue speaketh not unto men, but unto God: for no man understandeth him; howbeit in the spirit he speaketh mysteries.**
>
> **1 Corinthians 14:2**

Speaking in tongues allows you to speak mysteries or, literally in the Greek, *divine secrets* to God. You are not speaking to man; you are speaking directly to God and you are discussing divine secrets!

He that speaketh in an unknown tongues edifieth himself; but he that prophesieth edifieth the church.
1 Corinthians 14:4

The word *edifieth* is the same word we use that means "to charge up like charging up a battery." Tongues will build you up! It will charge up your spirit. It will keep you in tune with the things of God.

I would that ye all spake with tongues.
1 Corinthians 14:5

Paul is telling the whole church that everyone in the church should be speaking in tongues.

For if I pray in an unknown tongue, my spirit prayeth, but my understanding is unfruitful.
What is it then? I will pray with the spirit, and I will pray with the understanding also: I will sing with the spirit, and I will sing with the understanding also.
1 Corinthians 14:14,15

Have you noticed that when you pray with your mind, sometimes your flesh tends to be selfish? When you pray in the Spirit, however, your spirit is communing with God Himself and the flesh is not given the opportunity to enter into the conversation.

Else when thou shalt bless with the spirit, how shall he that occupieth the room of the unlearned say Amen at thy giving of thanks, seeing he understandeth not what thou sayest?
For thou verily givest thanks well, but the other is not edified.
1 Corinthians 14:16,17

When you pray in the Spirit, you are blessing and giving thanks to Almighty God. Verse 17 tells us that we even give thanks well! In the next verse Paul almost sounds like he is bragging when he admits, **I thank my God, I speak with tongues more than ye all.**

> **In the law it is written, With men of other tongues and other lips will I speak unto this people; and yet for all that will they not hear me, saith the Lord.**
>
> **Wherefore tongues are for a sign, not to them that believe, but to them that believe not: but prophesying serveth not for them that believe not, but for them which believe.**
>
> 1 Corinthians 14:21,22

When you bring unsaved people to the church and they hear you speaking in tongues, most of them are convinced it is of God, supernatural. It is a sign for the unbeliever.

> **How is it then, brethren? when ye come together, every one of you hath a psalm, hath a doctrine, hath a tongue, hath a revelation, hath an interpretation. Let all things be done unto edifying.**
>
> 1 Corinthians 14:26

Tongues are for public manifestation during church services to be a blessing to others as well as for your own personal edification in your prayer life.

> **Wherefore, brethren, covet to prophesy, and forbid not to speak with tongues.**
>
> **Let all things be done decently and in order.**
>
> 1 Corinthians 14:39,40

We are commanded in this verse not to forbid speaking in tongues. Every believer should be able to partake of this powerful blessing. Jude 20,21 tell us, **But ye, beloved, building up yourselves on your most holy faith, praying in the Holy Ghost, Keep yourselves in the love of God, looking for the mercy of our Lord Jesus Christ unto eternal life.** The ability to speak in tongues is also a tool to help build you up for everyday living in the secular world. It strengthens you to rise above *all* things that try to come against you.

Over the last twenty years of ministry, I have guided hundreds of people in receiving the infilling of the Holy Spirit. We don't have to ask God to send the Holy Ghost, because He is here. He has been with us since the Day of Pentecost. All we have to do is *receive Him*. We receive Him just like we receive salvation and healing. We don't have to ask God to send salvation to us. Neither do we need to ask for the sending of His Holy Spirit. He sent Him two thousand years ago, along with our salvation. All we have to do is receive Him.

Often we say "Brother So-and-so got saved last night." No, he got saved two thousand years ago; he *received* salvation last night. Isn't that right? The same thing is true with the Holy Spirit. Some people imagine that the Holy Ghost is going to make them lose control. They think He is going to grab their tongue, pull it out about three feet and make them say, "blahhhhh." He is *not* going to do that! If we wait for Him to do that, we are not going to receive.

What is the Bible method of receiving the Holy Ghost?

> **And they were all filled with the Holy Ghost, and began to speak with other tongues,** *as the Spirit gave them utterance.*
>
> **Acts 2:4**

When you are full of the Holy Ghost, you will begin to speak. Does the Word say they got filled with the Holy Ghost, and the Holy Ghost talked for them? No. Did it say the Holy Ghost yanked their tongues and made them speak? No. It says they got filled with the Holy Ghost, and *they began to speak.*

The believers started speaking. This means they opened their mouths and said something. Notice, **the Spirit gave them utterance.** The Holy Ghost gives us the words, but we do the talking. When you keep repeating, "Father, I want to receive the Holy Ghost. Thank You, Jesus, thank You, Jesus, thank You, Jesus, oh, thank You, Jesus," or you say, "Father, I want to receive the Holy Ghost," and then you clam up frozen in fear, you are not in a position to receive. The Holy Spirit is a gentleman, and He won't just take over. You have to *receive* Him. So, if you close your mouth or if you keep talking in English, you are not going to receive. You have to open your mouth to speak.

I tell believers all the time, "Just begin to speak; don't talk in English." They say, "Well, how do I do that?" Guidance is the Holy Spirit's job. He gives the utterance. You receive this experience by faith, the same as salvation. By faith you open your mouth and trust God to give you the utterance. God's Spirit gives the language as He fills you. Simply yield to Him, receive Him and let those words come out from your belly. Out of your belly will flow rivers of living water. They will come up from your spirit, flow out over your vocal cords and you will speak in other tongues. Amen!

Chapter Three
Benefits of Speaking in Tongues

We have endeavored to establish that speaking in tongues is a valid Bible experience for us today. So the next question you may be asking is, "What is the purpose or benefit of speaking in tongues? If this is so beneficial, how can we increase the manifestations of the gifts of the Spirit in our lives and in our services?"

It Is Okay to Covet God's Stuff!

But covet earnestly the best gifts: and yet shew I unto you a more excellent way.

1 Corinthians 12:31

Notice, it says to *covet* these gifts. When you hear the word *covet*, you may think of it in a negative connotation. Paul is telling us to covet earnestly the best gifts. We should be coveting, or longing for, the gifts which best suit our needs at any given moment.

But the manifestation of the Spirit is given to every man to profit withal.

For to one is given by the Spirit the word of wisdom; to another the word of knowledge by the same Spirit;

To another faith by the same Spirit; to another the gifts of healing by the same Spirit;

To another the working of miracles; to another prophecy; to another discerning of spirits; to another divers kinds of tongues; to another the interpretation of tongues:

But all these worketh that one and the selfsame Spirit, dividing to every man severally as he will.

1 Corinthians 12:7-11

Paul lets us know from Scripture that there are different spiritual gifts at work within the body of Christ. Some might be considered more important because they are listed first, but all are essential. These manifestations of the Spirit are given to Christians to profit the entire body. And they do, as long as they are exercised in love.

> **Follow after charity, and desire spiritual gifts, but rather that ye may prophesy.**
>
> **1 Corinthians 14:1**

Scripture not only tells us to desire spiritual gifts and to follow after love, it also tells us that God desires His believers to covet prophesying. If you are longing for something, it would be appropriate to pray for it. In other words, it is appropriate to pray for these gifts to be in manifestation in our lives. However, you would want to pray unselfishly, "Lord, I am available, but if You want to use someone else, use them, because I want the gifts to be in manifestation so the whole church will be blessed." You desire the gifts to be in manifestation for the benefit of the whole Body of Christ.

On the other hand, some believers think that by praying in this unselfish manner, they will not be used by God. Since *coveting* has always had negative implications (i.e., do not covet your neighbor's things!), many of us are afraid to pray for spiritual gifts. We feel we are wrong to be coveting. But we are not wrong to covet the things of God as long as He is glorified. So, what do you do after you pray for the best gifts? You long after them. You want them. You desire them. You think of ways to receive them.

We should desire to have the gifts of the Spirit as well as the ministry gifts. This is the very attitude that the Holy Ghost wants you to have concerning spiritual gifts. He wants you to long for them, to desire them and to pursue them. He wants them to be brought into greater manifestation in your own life.

Then the Holy Ghost throws the icing on the cake when He says, "I want you to prophesy." We know from another verse that we can all prophesy one by one (1 Corinthians 14:31). This gift operates at one time or another in every believer's life, especially when witnessing.

Often, as you speak to someone about Jesus, suddenly you hear yourself speaking eloquently about the grace of God. As you hear yourself talking, you think, "I never knew that. I never saw it quite that way before." If you stay quiet and appear as if this is normal for you, they will think you know much more than you actually do! Little do they know that you are hearing it for the first time.

This is prophecy in operation. In a simple form, yes, but it is *inspired utterance*. It comes up from the inside, from your spirit man.

How to Develop the Gifts in Your Life

For I say, through the grace given unto me, to every man that is among you, not to think of himself more highly than he ought to think; but to think soberly, according as God hath dealt to every man the measure of faith.

Romans 12:3

This verse indicates that all believers start out with the same amount of faith. No one receives more faith than another. We all start at the same level, then it is up to us to do something with our faith. We can develop our faith. We can either build it, or lose it. One time Jesus said to His disciples, **Where is your faith?** (Luke 8:25). Obviously, they had lost it for a little while. We can have strong faith or weak faith, but we all start out with the same measure.

Having then gifts differing according to the grace that is given to us, whether prophecy, let us prophesy according to the proportion of faith.

Romans 12:6

61

In the same way you develop your faith by continually stepping out and acting on the promises of God, the more you yield to the Holy Spirit on the inside of you and let Him speak forth in tongues, interpretation of tongues, and prophecy, the more you will be used in a public service in this manner.

Have you ever sat in a service when there was a time of quiet reverence toward God? This is a time when you have sung from your heart. You have sung in the Spirit and then you are quiet and you wait. During this time, have you ever heard words in your spirit, or felt a strong pounding on the inside, and asked yourself, "Is this God or is this just me? What are these words. Is this for me or is this for everyone?"

If your faith is developed in the area of operating in the spiritual gifts, you will know. If it is not developed yet, the best way to develop your faith in regard to prophecy is to begin practicing during prayer in your own private devotions. It doesn't matter whether it's praying in tongues or praying in your understanding. Wait on God, and do whatever He is leading you to do.

Speaking to yourselves in psalms and hymns and spiritual songs, singing and making melody in your heart to the Lord.

Ephesians 5:19

This is interpreted to mean that you speak and sing to one another and to yourselves. Most spiritual things can develop in private. You can be taught, instructed and become accustomed to flowing with the Holy Ghost in your own personal devotions. If we don't spend time privately with God, then we wander aimlessly through life learning through trial and error.

Remember, Paul said, "I will show you a better way" (1 Corinthians 12:31). The Lord wants to manifest Himself in greater ways than in tongues and interpretation of tongues, although these gifts will be manifested the most. Because tongues and interpretation of tongues are distinct to this dispensation in time, these gifts will be more prominent.

Prophecy means to speak under the inspiration of the Holy Spirit, on behalf of God. We should earnestly desire to prophesy, but prophecy in the believer's life does not mean we stand in the office of a prophet, or one who predicts or tells the future.

For example, remember when the Prophet Isaiah went to Hezekiah and said, **Set thine house in order: for thou shalt die, and not live** (Isaiah 38:1). This was changeable, or conditional, prophecy. When Hezekiah repented and cried out to God, the Lord heard his prayers, saw his tears and granted him fifteen more years of life. Thus, the prophet's prophecy of the future changed with God's mercy. (See verses 1-5 of Isaiah 38.)

Prophecy, or speaking under the inspiration of God, is a gift that can minister to others.

> **But the hour cometh, and now is, when the true worshippers shall worship the Father in spirit and in truth: for the Father seeketh such to worship him.**
> **God is a Spirit: and they that worship him must worship him in spirit and in truth.**
> **John 4:23,24**

Notice this phrase, **in spirit and in truth** and the phrase, **the Father seeketh such.** If you want God's attention, then you need to spend your time in worship to Him *in the truth of His Word* and *in the Spirit*. God responds to those who are well taught and grounded in conversing with Him in line with His Word.

Jesus went on to say, **God *is* a Spirit.** That word *is* here, is in italics. Since it is not really there in the Greek, it has been used for clarification. We could say "God a Spirit: and they that worship Him must worship in Spirit and truth." It is so important that we conscientiously live our lives as Spirit-filled believers, having Spirit-filled days, being in and of God's Spirit to know and worship Him.

How can we be comfortable with the Holy Spirit manifesting Himself if He only gets an opportunity to show up on Sundays and Wednesdays in our lives? You wouldn't be at ease with someone if you only spoke to them once in a great while. In other words, if you will learn to fellowship with the Father through the Person of the Holy Spirit on a day-in and day-out basis, then the matters of the Spirit will become much more clear to you and you will be much more comfortable with them.

How do you begin? The first step is to be filled with the Holy Ghost. You might ask, "How do I know if I am filled with the Holy Ghost?" If you speak in tongues, then you have been. If you don't speak in tongues, then you are not filled with the Holy Ghost. The initial evidence of being filled with the Holy Ghost is the ability to speak with other tongues.

It never ceases to amaze me the amount of people who go to Word churches (charismatic churches or faith churches — whatever you want to call them) and enjoy the services and the teaching, but never make the decision to receive the infilling of the Holy Ghost. They have a lot of reasons. They may be scared or unsure if it is for them. Maybe they just want to listen to the preaching. But God is after our worship unto Him in Spirit and in truth.

The starting point in the Spirit-filled life is to be filled with the Holy Ghost with the evidence of speaking in tongues. Ephesians 5:18 says we should be in a state of *being filled* — a constant experience of being filled to overflowing with the presence of God.

When I got out of Bible school, I *cut my teeth* in the ministry in a Pentecostal church. These people believed in the Holy Ghost. They believed in answering an altar call to receive this experience. They also believed in *swarming*. At the altar, people swarmed over the converts and screamed in tongues. They would say, "Press through, hold on, let go" — all that sort of stuff. Then, if a person did receive, the swarmers were through.

In talking with some of them, they were amazed that I spoke in tongues daily. Many of them had been filled with the Holy Ghost from five to twenty years, yet they hadn't spoken in tongues since their initial infilling. It is true they were filled at one time, that they had received this experience, but they aren't filled with the Holy Ghost today.

Do you own an automobile? Do you fill it up with gasoline sometime during the week? Your car may be only one-quarter full. That also means three-quarters empty!

Many Christians have done the same thing regarding the baptism of the Holy Spirit. This is not very different from what happened to me in a denominational church which was very evangelistically oriented. Their entire focus was on getting people saved. Then once they were saved, they were left to themselves. Every week the sermon was on salvation. Nothing more. It was as if you had *arrived* once you were saved.

Because we have been filled once doesn't mean we are filled today in the true sense of the word. Ephesians talks of *constantly being filled to overflowing.* Certainly, we have the Person of the Holy Ghost, but it is important to yield every day to allow Him to express Himself in our lives by spending time praying in other tongues.

The First Benefit of Speaking in Tongues Is Edification

Let's go back now to 1 Corinthians and look at some verses which re-emphasize the importance of praying in other tongues.

He that speaketh in an unknown tongue edifieth himself; but he that prophesieth edifieth the church.

1 Corinthians 14:4

65

I want you to notice the first half of this verse, **He that speaketh in an unknown tongue edifies himself.** That is, he builds himself up or charges himself. W. E. Vine's *Expository Dictionary* relates this experience to a *charging up*. The analogy is like putting jumper cables on a battery that is low and charging it back up. It is still a battery, and it still has some juice to it, but we can charge that juice and make it stronger!

It is the same thing when we speak in tongues. Speaking in tongues will edify and build up our inner man. So why don't we do this daily? Many of us don't like to spend a lot of time praying in tongues because our mind wanders from project to project. We can think of a million other things that need to be done. Our mind likes to be in control of our body, so it distracts our spirit man by meandering, because it is untrained.

How can you get your mind trained? Romans 12:2 tells us, **be ye transformed by the renewing of your mind.** You renew your mind by meditating on the Scriptures, reading and thinking about the Word of God. When you do, here is what happens: Number one, you are being obedient to the Word of God by meditating on it. And number two, your inner man is being built up by speaking in tongues. Your mind doesn't necessarily have to understand that process.

For instance, when you eat right and exercise consistently, your physical body will function better, but your mind doesn't have to comprehend all the medical reasons why it is so. Isn't that right? What I am saying is that it doesn't matter if your mind understands the physiological concepts or not. You still get good results if you apply good principles.

The same thing is true in the spirit realm. You renew your mind through studying the Scriptures, while you build up your inner man by conversing with God through the Holy Ghost. First Corinthians 14:4 tells us that by doing this we receive the benefit of edification, or being built up. We apply a good principle and get good results because the Bible says it is so—not necessarily because we know how or why it works. *The Amplified Version* of 1 Corinthians 14:14 says:

> For if I pray in an [unknown] tongue, my spirit [by the Holy Spirit within me] prays, but my mind is unproductive [it bears no fruit and helps nobody].

Notice, the double negative in this verse. With regard to praying by the Holy Spirit, Paul is saying, "Okay, my mind is blank and it is not helping anybody." Then in verse 15 he says, "What am I going to do?" The solution follows when Paul declares, **I will pray with the spirit, and I will pray with the understanding also: I will sing with the spirit, and I will sing with the understanding also.**

In other words, Paul is going to do both. He will pray and sing to God in the Spirit (by the Holy Spirit within him) and in truth (with his intelligence and his understanding) in order to edify unbelievers, the Church, and himself.

The Second Benefit of Speaking in Tongues Is Giving Thanks Well

> **Else when thou shalt bless with the spirit, how shall he that occupieth the room of the unlearned say Amen at thy giving of thanks, seeing he understandeth not what thou sayest?**
>
> **For thou verily givest thanks well, but the other is not edified.**
>
> **1 Corinthians 14:16,17**

Paul tells us that we benefit by praying in tongues and singing in tongues because we are giving thanks well. Someone inevitably asks, "Giving thanks for what?"

Maybe I am thanking God for the air I am breathing, for the church I enjoy, for the home He has provided for me, and for the family that He has given me. Perhaps I am verbalizing gratitude for the health that flows through my body or for the finances that He has blessed me with. Possibly I am expressing appreciation to God for His angels all about me who protect me and to bear me up in their hands so I won't get hurt. It could be that I am thanking God for what He is going to do in the future, or that I have escaped hell and I am going to heaven. The Bible says I am giving thanks well, and that should be motivation enough to continue to pray in the Spirit.

Do you like to give your children things? Don't you just swell up with pride when they say "thank you"? When our children on their own say thank you for something we did, it makes us so happy.

In some ways our relationship with our children is like our relationship with Father God. When we speak in tongues, we could simply be thanking Him for being our Father or for having imparted eternal life into our spirit. It is worth speaking in tongues every day, isn't it? The more comfortable you get with speaking in tongues, the more comfortable you get in the realm of the Spirit. And the more comfortable you get in the realm of the Spirit, the more apt you become to have spiritual gifts manifest in your life.

The Third Benefit of Speaking in Tongues Is Assurance and Relationship

As we become freer in our spiritual communication, and our spiritual walk with the Lord becomes more intimate, we can look to our Father for comfort. Let's take a look into *how* fellowship with our God can enrich our well-being.

And I will pray the Father, and he shall give you another Comforter, that he may abide with you for ever;

Even the Spirit of truth; whom the world cannot receive, because it seeth him not, neither knoweth him: but ye know him; for he dwelleth with you, and shall be in you.

I will not leave you comfortless: I will come to you.
John 14:16-18

Aren't you glad the Holy Ghost is a Comforter and not a punisher? We can embrace this passage of Scripture, accept it in faith, and bask in the truth of it. The Holy Ghost is with us. Jesus said that He would never leave us or forsake us. He said that He would send us another Comforter. He said He would come to us in the Person of the Holy Ghost and that He would never leave us comfortless.

The world cannot receive Him and doesn't even know Him. But we know Him. He is with us, and He is in us. He will abide with us forever. We can take these verses, hold on to them and enjoy them. But there is something about praying in the Holy Ghost that makes these promises even more real. When you are speaking in tongues it reminds, assures and reinforces the presence of the Holy Ghost in your life.

As a denominational believer, I constantly got myself into situations where the devil would tell me, "That's it...you have lost your salvation." Have you ever been there? My church taught that we couldn't lose our salvation, but at times I thought I did anyway! I would get so depressed and discouraged wondering whether it was so. After several months of this, I finally got filled with the Holy Ghost. I knew Scripture even as a denominational person. I knew Jesus said He would never leave me or forsake me. And I knew that according to what we believed, I couldn't lose my salvation. Still, I was in doubt.

Have you ever wondered? I mean, when you really mess up and the devil tells you that you have lost it?

Driving down the road one day after messing up completely by losing my temper, the devil said to me, "It's gone. You might as well quit trying to do right. You might as well start going back to the bars and to your old lifestyle. You might as well quit going to church. It's not doing you any good. You're a hypocrite. You're a liar."

Satan's lies and deceit always get worse. However, when we understand the Word of God, the good news is that Jesus tells us how to beat him. It is not that people who go to church don't face problems, by any stretch of the imagination. We are just smarter, or we should be, because we have found the Answer to our problems!

When I got filled with the Holy Ghost, I found out the truth. No one taught me; it came to me from the inside. When I lost my temper and released a bunch of words I shouldn't have said, I started feeling bad.

The devil said, "That's it. You got filled with the Holy Ghost. You thought that was the *cure-all* for everything. Yet, in just a few weeks, here you are losing your temper." He had me. I *did* do it. Then he said, "You are not worthy to be called a Christian. There is no cure-all. This stuff is all in your head. It can't possibly be real." As I sat there listening, he continued, "Really, you have lost your salvation this time. You're on a sliding board on your way out, sliding downhill. Actually, God doesn't want you back now because you are even worse. He trusted you with this Holy Ghost experience, and you let Him down by losing your temper."

I am thinking about what the devil is saying which makes it even worse. I feel my spirit man getting smaller and smaller inside me as I am driving down the road. Then suddenly, it came to me. If I had lost my salvation this time, certainly I wouldn't be able to speak in tongues anymore. So I figured I might as well give it a try. It wasn't a real big spiritual revelation. I opened my mouth and started speaking in tongues. Then I said with confidence, "Devil, you are a liar. I didn't lose my salvation. I can still speak in tongues."

That experience began to do something to me. It wasn't that I went out and lost my temper on purpose after that. Let's just say that I had plenty of opportunities to make other mistakes. And when I did, the devil would cast doubt on my salvation. So I would speak in tongues. When I spoke in tongues, it confirmed that I was still saved, and slow but sure, the devil quit using the argument against me.

More than twenty years have come and gone since then, and never again has the devil tried to tell me I have lost my salvation. Yet, in that first year, the devil reminded me hundreds of times that there was no hope for me.

I am telling you about my experience so you can see that speaking in tongues not only gives you assurance of the closeness of God, but that it is also a reminder of your relationship with Him in the presence of the Comforter. He is here to help us by showing us the way back to God. He is here to point us to the blood of Jesus Christ, to confession and repentance of sin, to a victorious, overcoming life!

The Fourth Benefit of Speaking in Tongues Is Rest and Refreshing

Just as speaking in tongues can bring assurance and comfort in our relationship with the Lord, God promised through the prophet Isaiah that it also brings rest and refreshing.

> **For precept must be upon precept, precept upon precept; line upon line, line upon line; here a little, and there a little:**
>
> **For with stammering lips and another tongue will he speak to this people.**

> To whom he said, This is the rest wherewith ye may cause the weary to rest; and this is the refreshing: yet they would not hear.
>
> Isaiah 28:10-12

Notice, **with stammering lips and another tongue will he speak to this people.** He calls this *rest* and *refreshing*.

Speaking in tongues is a refreshing from the cares of this world. It is also a relief not to say the same old stale prayers that beg and squall and bawl for God to do something. Just throw those prayers aside, begin to pray in other tongues, and be rejuvenated in the presence of God! Let the Holy Spirit through your spirit express Himself to God. Someone might ask, "Will that do me any good?" More than you can ever imagine!

The Fifth Benefit of Speaking in Tongues Is Holy Spirit Intercession

> Likewise the Spirit also helpeth our infirmities (now that's not sicknesses, but weaknesses): **for we know not what we should pray for as we ought: but the Spirit itself maketh intercession for us with groanings which cannot be uttered** (or put into regular words).
>
> And he that searcheth the hearts knoweth what is the mind of the Spirit, because he maketh intercession for the saints according to the will of God.
>
> And we know that all things work together for good to them that love God, to them who are the called according to his purpose.
>
> Romans 8:26-28

Praying in tongues, or praying in the Holy Ghost, keeps us praying in line with the Word of God, especially in situations where we don't know how or what to pray.

I have seen believers who were filled with the Holy Ghost at one time, but neglected to keep up their relationship with God. Still, when an emergency arises or they get in a jam, instantly tongues come flying out of them. Why? Mainly, because they have enough sense to know they are in trouble, and they have no answers or resources to get out of it.

In spite of this, they are usually not in a confident enough position to pray for the troubling situation as they ought. When you are praying in faith, you can have confidence.

> **And this is the confidence that we have in him, that, if we ask any thing according to his will, he heareth us:**
>
> **And if we know that he hear us, whatsoever we ask, we know that we have the petitions that we desired of him.**
>
> **1 John 5:14,15**

Receiving what we desire is based on our having confidence in the will and Word of God, which are one and the same. If we are in sin, backslidden or in a very shallow relationship with God, we won't have that confidence. I am persuaded this is why believers call their friends to pray for them. They don't have confidence in their own prayers.

Without confidence, we are not in a position to pray for something as we should. To restore our fellowship with God, we need to repent. Then, we need to build up our own confidence level in the Word of God by remembering that He has forgiven us and washed away our sins. Though our transgressions were red as scarlet, after forgiveness, they are white as snow. The memory of the offense has even been cast into the sea of forgetfulness, and we are once again clothed in the robe of righteousness. We are standing before God as if we had never sinned.

It is easier for someone who has active fellowship with God to accept forgiveness than someone who has a shallow relationship with Him. Automatically, they will pray in the

Holy Ghost when they don't know how or what to pray. We can be sure that the Holy Ghost will always make intercession for us, or through us, as He prays the perfect prayer.

Naturally, there are other times when we attempt to have a perfect relationship with God and still get ourselves in a situation in which we don't know exactly how to pray as we should.

In my own personal life, 90 percent of my prayer life is in tongues. I pray more in English in my church than I do at home. Praying in English is for the benefit of the entire church body so we can all agree with what we are praying.

I found out years ago that by praying in tongues I got a lot more accomplished, experienced a lot more spiritual activity, and had more visitations of God in my life than I ever did when praying in English. Of course that doesn't negate praying in English. If we have a specific need and we know what God's Word says in that area, we need to pray according to His Word. We can't just throw it all off on the Holy Ghost and say, "I am not going to learn about different kinds of prayer — I am just going to pray this way all the time."

But as we begin to pray in line with God's Word, we will be amazed at how things will work out. If you are in a certain situation that you don't know how to pray for as you should, you can simply say, "Lord, I don't know how to pray about this particular area, this specific direction or this special situation. I really do not know how to pray anymore. So right now, as an act of my will, I am going to rely on You. I am going to pray in the Holy Ghost and I am trusting You that this situation will be addressed and be resolved."

At times I don't have a clue as to how God will answer in a certain circumstance; that is, unless He gives me the interpretation. I just say out loud, "I am going to trust You to help me pray in the Spirit about this problem, about this

person, about this relationship, about this obstacle —
whatever it is — the way You know that it needs to be
prayed." Then I yield myself to God and begin to pray in
tongues until the Lord gives me the interpretation, or I have
a sense of release.

There is great reassurance in knowing you can pray in
the Holy Ghost about everything. You can't excuse your
responsibility to pray in English, but when you get to a
place where you don't know how to pray, you should
always pray in tongues.

When we are dealing with people and their problems as
pastors, we *never* know if we are getting the whole story. We
can be convinced during our counseling conversations that
we know the whole truth and that we know exactly how to
pray. Then another little variation pops up. Many times I
start off praying, "Lord, You know they have asked for
prayer. This is what they have said, still I am not sure I have
the entire story, so I am just going to trust You to help me
pray."

In my own life sometimes I think I have the purest
motives, but then I start asking myself, "Wait just a minute.
What is the root cause? What do I want to accomplish? Why
do I want to accomplish this?" Maybe you never question
yourself, but I do. I just say, "Lord, now help me. If I am
praying amiss to consume it on my own lusts, help me,
show me. I am going to roll this one over on the Holy
Ghost. I am going to pray in tongues and, therefore, pray
for it accurately and rightly."

God's Word works, but if we never spend time praying
in tongues, if we do all our praying in English, then we are
not fulfilling what Jesus said in the gospel of John.

> **But the hour cometh, and now is, when the true
> worshippers shall worship the Father in spirit and in
> truth: for the Father seeketh such to worship him.**
>
> **John 4:23**

You need to stay in the middle of the road on this. When you join a Spirit-filled church, you need to get filled with the Holy Ghost. When you get there, you will already be labeled a *fanatic*. So why not just get it all? Then once you are filled with the Holy Ghost, you must not lay Him to the side. Don't say, "Well, that was fun, shun da le hie," and never do it again. No, make a commitment to talk in tongues each day. Take my word for it. You will become more familiar and comfortable with the things of the Spirit by praying every day in the Holy Ghost. It is then that you will have more manifestations of the Spirit in your own life.

The Sixth Benefit of Speaking in Tongues Is Spirit Communication

It is awesome when God manifests Himself in the church! He wants to do that. He wants to show Himself strong on behalf of His people. But it is even more exciting when you are going about your daily business and He shares personal things with you.

How about when you are lying in bed at night falling asleep, and suddenly, you have to wake up because your spirit man is praying in tongues in the back of your consciousness! You open your eyes and you hear praying on the inside and say, "What's going on? You're talking without me."

These are exciting times in God. He can tell us things to come and we can jump right in on the conversation. I am thoroughly convinced God does much of His talking to the spirit of most believers at night when they are asleep. Perhaps it's because some of us are not quiet enough during the day. Maybe we are too busy to listen to Him. Your spirit never sleeps.

Years ago, we taught a course to our congregation called, *How to be Led by the Spirit and How to Develop Your*

Spirit Man. Some people thought I made some of it up. Then the *doers* confirmed the teaching by giving me testimonies of the truths that were taught.

We can train the human spirit! I have told people, "You don't need an alarm clock, just go home and do this: Say out loud to your spirit man, 'Spirit, you never sleep. In the name of Jesus I am talking to you. Wake me up at seven o'clock (or six o'clock or five o'clock or whatever).'" And he will. I am not talking about God. I am talking about your spirit on the inside.

To develop this communication with my spirit man I would say things like, "Wake me up at seven minutes after six or three minutes after six o'clock." My eyes would come open in the morning right on time. What makes this even more amazing is that my clock is always about five minutes off. But our spirit isn't baffled by that. He knows which clock we are going to look at when we open our eyes.

The born again human spirit is already in contact with God, but if we will learn to speak in tongues through the Holy Ghost, we will be in contact with God even more. We will be more accessible and usable to manifest spiritual gifts in the church to be a blessing to God's people.

For he that speaketh in an unknown tongue speaketh not unto men, but unto God: for no man understandeth him; howbeit in the spirit he speaketh mysteries (or divine secrets).
1 Corinthians 14:2

I have heard believers say that tongues are really a *hot line.* I don't know about that. But we certainly have a direct connection to heaven when we speak in our heavenly language — a language that discusses *divine secrets,* or divine mysteries, between our spirit, the Holy Spirit within us, and God the Father!

The Seventh Benefit of Speaking in Tongues Is Keeping the Tongue in Subjection to God

But the tongue can no man tame; it is an unruly evil, full of deadly poison.

James 3:8

James says that no man can keep the tongue in subjection. It is an unruly evil. However, speaking in tongues keeps it in subjection. The more time we spend speaking in tongues, the less time we have for our mouths to say the things that get us in trouble. Then we become more conscious of our speech and our obedience to God!

It is worth doing! It is beneficial and valuable! Take time every day to speak in tongues and become more acquainted with the Holy Ghost. Your spiritual life will become richer if you do.

Chapter Four
Holy Ghost Manifestations

In this chapter I want to share with you some of the manifestations of God found in the Bible. I will also give some insight into some of the observations I have made over the years.

> **And he said, I beseech thee, shew me thy glory.**
>
> **And he said, I will make all my goodness pass before thee, and I will proclaim the name of the Lord before thee; and will be gracious to whom I will be gracious, and will shew mercy on whom I will show mercy.**
>
> **And he said, Thou canst not see my face: for there shall no man see me, and live.**
>
> **And the Lord said, Behold, there is a place by me, and thou shalt stand upon a rock:**
>
> **And it shall come to pass, while my glory passeth by, that I will put thee in a clift of the rock, and will cover thee with my hand while I pass by:**
>
> **And I will take away mine hand, and thou shalt see my back parts: but my face shall not be seen.**
>
> **Exodus 33:18-23**

In this passage of Scripture, Moses asked to see God's glory. But God told him no person could look upon God's face and live, because God's glory is too powerful and holy to be looked upon with human eyes. However, God allowed Moses to see His back parts as He passed by.

> **And he was there with the Lord forty days and forty nights; he did neither eat bread, nor drink water. And**

he wrote upon the tables the words of the covenant, the ten commandments.

And it came to pass, when Moses came down from mount Sinai with the two tables of testimony in Moses' hand, when he came down from the mount, that Moses wist not that the skin of his face shone while he talked with him.

And when Aaron and all the children of Israel saw Moses, behold, the skin of his face shone; and they were afraid to come nigh him.

And Moses called unto them; and Aaron and all the rulers of the congregation returned unto him: and Moses talked with them.

And afterward all the children of Israel came nigh: and he gave them in commandment all that the Lord had spoken with him in mount Sinai.

And till Moses had done speaking with them, he put a vail in on his face.

But when Moses went in before the Lord to speak with him, he took the vail off, until he came out. And he came out, and spake unto the children of Israel that which he was commanded.

And the children of Israel saw the face of Moses, that the skin of Moses' face shone: and Moses put the vail upon his face again, until he went in to speak with him.

Exodus 34:28-35

Some of these verses point out that Moses' face *glowed*. (What would our churches think today if we started getting some of these *neon-faced* believers in our services?) So many things can happen when a believer comes in contact with the anointing of God.

But if the ministration of death, written and engraven in stones, was glorious, so that the children of Israel could not stedfastly behold the face of Moses for the glory of his countenance; which glory was to be done away:

How shall not the ministration of the spirit be rather glorious?

For if the ministration of condemnation be glory, much more doth the ministration of righteousness exceed in glory.

For even that which was made glorious had no glory in this respect, by reason of the glory that excelleth.

For if that which is done away was glorious, much more that which remaineth is glorious.

Seeing then that we have such hope, we use great plainness of speech:

And not as Moses, which put a vail over his face, that the children of Israel could not stedfastly look to the end of that which is abolished:

But their minds were blinded: for until this day remaineth the same vail untaken away in the reading of the old testament; which vail is done away in Christ.

But even unto this day, when Moses is read, the vail is upon their heart.

Nevertheless when it shall turn to the Lord, the vail shall be taken away.

Now the Lord is that Spirit: and where the Spirit of the Lord is, there is liberty.

But we all, with open face beholding as in a glass the glory of the Lord, are changed into the same image from glory to glory, even as by the Spirit of the Lord.

2 Corinthians 3:7-18

In Exodus when Moses asked to see God's face, he was told that he could see another part of God's body, but not His face. The face of God represents His glory. Second Corinthians 3:18 says, **...we all, with open face beholding as in a glass the glory of the Lord.** Second Corinthians 3:8 also says the same thing. Jesus Christ made it possible for us to behold God's face — His glory — by supernatural acts of the Holy Spirit being manifested in the natural realm. To witness this glory, tradition must be forsaken. When we become fervent in Spirit and pure in heart, we will see the greatest moves and manifestations of God ever witnessed on earth. Why?

> **The glory of this latter house shall be greater than of the former, saith the Lord of hosts: and in this place will I give peace, saith the Lord of hosts.**
>
> **Haggai 2:9**

God's glory is revealed in Jesus.

> **For God, who commanded the light to shine out of darkness, hath shined in our hearts, to give the light of the knowledge of the glory of God in the face of Jesus Christ.**
>
> **2 Corinthians 4:6**

The Bible is full of God's brilliance. We can turn the power and glory of God loose by believing the Word of God with all sincerity, reality and confidence. To do this we must be assured that God's Word is true. And most importantly, we have to act on, or be obedient to His Word.

When dealing with manifestations of the Holy Ghost, one question that often comes up is, "Why do people fall under the power? Is this experience in the Bible?" The Bible clearly answers this question, but one minister I know answers it well by saying, "When the natural comes in contact with the supernatural, something has to give. Before answering this question from the Bible, however, let it be forever settled in your mind: it does not matter whether a person falls or does not fall; God is still God."

Sometimes when the natural comes in contact with the supernatural, a person loses their ability to stand up, so they fall. Other times, an individual will not fall, but his equilibrium may be greatly affected. A biblical example of this is reported in Acts where Peter describes the events on the Day of Pentecost.

> **For these are not drunken, as ye suppose, seeing it is but the third hour of the day.**
>
> **Acts 2:15**

A drunk person has trouble walking or even standing. On occasion, I have witnessed some believers' unsteadiness under the incredible power of God as they weave and stagger around. Balance is not intact, but neither do they fall down. I have seen a number just stumble around like a drunk. An experience such as this is a manifestation of the Spirit of God as recorded in Acts 2.

There are numerous ways in the Scriptures that people reacted to the manifestations of God's presence. One time a person's voice was affected by the Spirit of God.

In Luke's gospel, Zechariah did not believe Gabriel when he told him that a child would be born unto him (Luke 1:5-22). Gabriel is an angel of significance. He is the one who says, "I stand in the very presence of God." As a result, Zechariah, who initially did not accept the presence of God or the messenger of God, was struck dumb and could not speak until his son was born.

I have personally experienced times when hands were laid on believers and they could not resume speaking in English for a long period of time after starting to speak in tongues.

To give more examples of the reality of the manifested presence of God's Spirit and the way it affects people, take time to read the book, *Signs and Wonders,* by Maria Woodworth-Etter published by Harrison House.

Maria Woodworth-Etter, an evangelist, in 1885, only fifteen years prior to our century, began a supernatural ministry. Around 1920 in St. Louis, Missouri, while in the middle of delivering a message, she was giving an illustration to make a point. As she raised her hand with her mouth open to do so, suddenly, the Spirit of God came on her and she froze in that position for three days and three nights. Her bodily functions stopped!

It is said that thousands of people attested to this account. All the newspapers in St. Louis photographed her. An estimated 150,000 people came from all over the country as soon as word of this incident became public to get a glimpse of this sister, frozen in this pose. Not only had her bodily functions ceased, but her eyes were not watering; they were simply open.

Then almost exactly to the hour, when the third night ended, she came back. She did not realize any time had expired. In fact, Maria Woodworth-Etter thought she was in the same meeting and continued with the point she was making prior to being suspended. Testimony to this being the most powerful ministry in the United States, and certainly in modern times, has been given.

In another incident reported in *Signs and Wonders* where Maria Woodworth-Etter was ministering under the anointing of God, a group of scoffers came and stood on the side of the tent. When they did, she pointed her finger at them and exercised her authority as a believer. Not only were the scoffers *slain in the Spirit* (actually, they fell over before God), their horses also collapsed under the power of God!

In the following Scriptures from Luke's gospel we see that the natural, human function of talking can be suspended by the presence of God.

> And Zacharias said unto the angel, Whereby shall I know this? for I am an old man, and my wife well stricken in years.
>
> And the angel answering said unto him, I am Gabriel, that stand in the presence of God; and am sent to speak unto thee, and to shew thee these glad tidings.
>
> And, behold, thou shalt be dumb, and not able to speak, until the day that these things shall be

performed, because thou believest not my words, which shall be fulfilled in their season.

Luke 1:18-20

And he asked for a writing table, and wrote, saying, His name is John. And they marvelled all.

And his mouth was opened immediately, and his tongue loosed, and he spake, and praised God.

Luke 1:63,64

This kind of supernatural manifestation happened in my own life in Berlin, Germany. My wife and I had walked into what we thought was a Bible study that turned out to be a transfer of leadership of that church to me. I became the pastor when the Lord spoke by the Spirit in a prayer circle saying, "Turn around and start ministering to these people under My anointing."

But I said, "I am not going to do it. I don't know anybody here. It's not my service."

So God said it again, "Turn around and minister to these people under My anointing."

I said, "No, You have to make a way. I am not going to do that."

Then the wife of the couple that started the church in their home walked up and stood in front of me and said, "The Lord just told me that He told you to do something and you are supposed to be obedient. Here is your permission."

When that happened, I was quick to move out and obey. I began to minister to the people. Then after a while, God said, "Stop." So I stopped.

Because the leadership of the church had been praying and were convinced that we were sent of God to them, they decided to lay hands on Kelly and me. They proceeded to turn the church over to us. And when hands were laid on me, it was as if I had been hit with fire. Though I did not fall down, I staggered back very hard. While staggering, I was able to find a chair and sat down as they continued to minister to me.

For one hour I could not speak in tongues or talk in English. I could write, but I could not talk. So I spent the next hour simply listening and writing down what I heard God speaking to my spirit.

When the natural comes in contact with the supernatural, the supernatural will prevail. We need to increase our vision of what God's Spirit will do and not limit ourselves to simply thinking people will fall (be slain in the Spirit) under the power of God.

Saul, who later become Paul, was knocked down by the power of God.

> **And Saul arose from the earth; and when his eyes were opened, he saw no man: but they led him by the hand, and brought him into Damascus.**
> **And he was three days without sight, and neither did eat nor drink.**
>
> **Acts 9:8,9**

Notice how his encounter with the presence of God affected him.

Paul heard Jesus' voice, was knocked down by His glory, saw a vision, stood up, and was unable to see. For three days and three nights he was blind.

A church member once asked me if it could have been normal for his vision to have become blurred while he was praying at the altar. Well, I believe Paul would have felt fortunate if his vision was only blurred, but according to Acts 8, he lost his sight completely!

John 18 records the moment that Judas, the Pharisees and the others came to apprehend Jesus to crucify Him. It also gives reference to a time in Scripture when people fell down under the power of God.

> **Jesus therefore, knowing all things that should come upon him, went forth, and said unto them, Whom seek ye?**
>
> **They answered him, Jesus of Nazareth. Jesus saith unto them, I am he. And Judas also, which betrayed him, stood with them.**
>
> **As soon then as he had said unto them, I am he, they went backward, and fell to the ground.**
>
> **John 18:4-6**

They went backward and fell to the ground. Jesus didn't even lay hands on them. They could not stand up in the presence of God. Jesus said, **He that hath seen me hath seen the Father** (John 14:9). In 2 Corinthians, we learned that we can see the glory of God by looking in the face of Jesus. The way we look in the face of Jesus is by looking in the Bible. I am amazed that this band of men had the audacity to arrest Jesus after falling backward under the power of God when in His presence.

Many of us have been praying for a greater outpouring of the supernatural in our midst. And God is certainly answering our prayers by moving dramatically. As we remain fervent in Spirit with full intensity, we are to do with all our might what the Spirit leads us to do.

If you think you have a word to prophesy, get up and prophesy with all your might. On the other hand, if you think you have a word, don't say, "I am not sure if this is God or not." The congregation will understand that you do not know if it is God or not. Instead, get up and say, "Here is what I have." Be enthusiastic about it! Let it out! Let the congregation judge it, receive it, or reject it.

Paul admonishes us in the book of Romans to be, **Not slothful in business; fervent in spirit; serving the Lord** (Romans 12:11). In other words, he tells us to keep the supernatural flowing.

Matthew tells us of certain Roman guards at Christ's burial site who started shaking for fear of an angel and became as dead men:

> And, behold, there was a great earthquake: for the angel of the Lord descended from heaven, and came and rolled back the stone from the door, and sat upon it.
>
> His countenance was like lightning, and his raiment white as snow:
>
> And for fear of him the keepers did shake, and became as dead men.
>
> **Matthew 28:2-4**

How do dead men look? Dead men don't stand; they lie down. Dead men don't move; they are out cold — literally cold! This Scripture says that when the angel, representing the presence of God, manifested at the resurrection of Jesus, he rolled back a stone and sat upon it. The angel did not touch the men. He did not breathe on them. He did not shoot lightning out of his fingertips. But these guards were in the presence of God in a sinful state. Their sinful state brought about great fear and conviction.

When we are born again, filled with the Spirit and walk cleansed by the blood of Jesus, there is no fear. There is joy! We get unrealistic ideas sometimes about what has to happen before anything supernatural takes place. The presence of the Lord will bring about the supernatural manifestations.

Every great revival of God has always been accompanied by people falling out under the power of God with supernatural signs and wonders.

Years ago, a religious group called Quakers was established. But a group called Shakers preceded the Quakers. The Shakers acquired their name because in their meetings, in times of preaching and moving in the Holy Ghost, they would start shaking, quivering and rolling around on the floor. This is how the term *Holy Roller* was derived. People shook, fell down and quivered, all under the power of God.

I heard Brother Hagin tell a story once about a meeting he attended when he saw the glory of God roll in like a mist or a cloud. It remained just above the congregation. When the people stood and raised their hands, upon impact with the cloud, their hands and arms began to shake as if electricity were going through them. As he tells it, at first, Brother Hagin thought the people were *putting on*. Since he could see the mist, he put his hand up in it too. And as soon as he did, his hand started shaking like everyone else's hands. So he pulled his hand down saying, "Well, maybe it is just nerves." Then he tried it with his other hand. But when he did, his other hand reacted the same way. So he put both hands up in the cloud, and both started shaking.

Not only do we have a scriptural precedent (2 Chronicles 5:14) for this, I am convinced there is more to the manifestations of the Holy Spirit than we (the Church world as a whole) know.

And after six days Jesus taketh Peter, James, and John his brother, and bringeth them up into an high mountain apart,

And was transfigured before them: and his face did shine as the sun, and his raiment was white as the light.

And, behold, there appeared unto them Moses and Elias talking with him.

Then answered Peter, and said unto Jesus, Lord, it is good for us to be here: if thou wilt, let us make here three tabernacles; one for thee, and one for Moses, and one for Elias.

While he yet spake, behold, a bright cloud overshadowed them: and behold a voice out of the cloud, which said, This is my beloved Son, in whom I am well pleased; hear ye him.

And when the disciples heard it, they fell on their face, and were sore afraid.

Matthew 17:1-6

Peter, James and John heard a voice that came from a cloud. It was God's voice. They fell on their faces and were afraid. No indication was given that these men fell down voluntarily; quite the contrary was implied.

And Jesus came and touched them, and said, Arise, and be not afraid.

Matthew 17:7

In Acts, Paul recounts his own *falling down* incident:

At midday, O king, I saw in the way a light from heaven, above the brightness of the sun, shining round about me and them which journeyed with me.

And when we were all fallen to the earth, I heard a voice speaking unto me, and saying in the Hebrew tongue, Saul, Saul, why persecutest thou me? it is hard for thee to kick against the pricks.

And I said, Who art thou, Lord? And he said, I am Jesus whom thou persecutest.

Acts 26:13-15

When we read of this occurrence in Acts 9 it does not mention Paul's companions falling, only Paul. In his account Paul said they all fell to the earth. It was not just Paul who was knocked down by the power of God, or slain in the Spirit, as it is also called. Paul's entire company experienced the manifested presence of God. God is a big God!

When we are astonished by God's power, something about us will change. Our voice, our ability to stand up, our ability to stay balanced, our vision, or our bodily functions change. These changes demonstrate being totally overwhelmed by God's power.

It is exciting to see people fall under the power of God, but wait until you witness God popping them up from the floor!

> **As the appearance of the bow that is in the cloud in the day of rain, so was the appearance of the brightness round about. This was the appearance of the likeness of the glory of the Lord. And when I saw it, I fell upon my face, and I heard a voice of one that spake.**
>
> Ezekiel 1:28
>
> **And he said unto me, Son of man, stand upon thy feet, and I will speak unto thee.**
>
> **And the spirit entered into me when he spake unto me, and set me upon my feet, that I heard him that spake unto me.**
>
> Ezekiel 2:1,2

Ezekiel had a supernatural vision and fell upon his face when he saw the glory of God. And he did not get up on his own. Ezekiel said in chapter 2, **The spirit entered into me when he spake unto me, and set me upon my feet, that I heard him that spake unto me**. There is more in the Bible than we think! We read the Bible too fast. We read so fast that we do not stop to think, "What *exactly* am I reading?"

Let me share something else from the ministry of Kenneth Hagin. He spoke of a particular brother in his church who never once missed dancing in the Spirit. When this brother would get up and dance in the Spirit, all kinds of things would start happening. It released an anointing.

Brother Hagin said that in one particular service while this man was dancing in the Spirit that he looked over and saw a lady in the congregation who had the power of God all over her. So he said, "Sister, get up and yield to that." Then the lady got up on the platform with him, closed her eyes, and started walking back and forth exhorting people to get saved.

The first fellow was still dancing on one side as this lady was walking back and forth exhorting people. Many in the congregation began praying and moaning; others began to get up and run to the platform to get saved. Every time someone would come to the altar to be saved, the woman would dance a little jig. And all this time her eyes were closed! She would know by the Spirit that someone had come up, then would dance a little jig for joy.

Brother Hagin commented, "It almost got distracting because she was going back and forth exhorting people to be saved with her eyes closed and just walking right up to the edge of the platform and turning." It was unsettling because some of the people just knew she was going to walk off the edge, but she turned every time. Finally, when the last person got saved, she started dancing under the Spirit of God. Now listen to this...Brother Hagin said that he, his wife, and over 100 other people all witnessed this woman dance right off the platform into mid-air, stand suspended in mid-air for a moment while dancing in the Spirit, then come right back onto the platform. At the sight of this *everyone* jumped out of the pews, came up to the front and worshipped God.

I am telling you, there is much more about the things of God that we don't know! Someone might say, "Wait a minute, you have gone too far. I am sorry but I just don't believe that." Well, let's go to the book of Acts, chapter 8. If you think it would be hard to dance *on air*, how about some transportation by the Spirit of God?

The Bible tells us about Philip. He had a great mass crusade beginning in Samaria, yet God knew there was one individual in another location who needed Philip. Philip had won practically an entire city to the Lord. But after returning to Jerusalem to continue preaching, an angel spoke to him and told him to go south.

Philip was obedient and joined himself to the Ethiopian eunuch's chariot. When he heard the man reading Isaiah, Philip ran over and asked if he understood what he was reading. When the man said, **How can I, except some man should guide me?** (Acts 8:31), Philip began from the point where the man was reading and preached Christ to him. The man was saved and baptized in water. But notice what happened next.

> **And when they were come up out of the water, the Spirit of the Lord caught away Philip, that the eunuch saw him no more: and he went on his way rejoicing.**

> **But Philip was found at Azotus: and passing through he preached in all the cities, till he came to Caesarea.**

> **Acts 8:39,40**

Philip was found in Azotus? In verse 39 *caught* is the same word used in 1 Thessalonians 4:17 in reference to the Rapture. In my interpretation, the Spirit said, "Okay, Philip, you are finished here. I'll lift you up in mid-air, bring you over and drop you off many miles away." Then Philip said, "Well, I find myself here in Azotus; so I guess I might as well keep on preaching!"

If we can believe Acts 8, it should not be too hard to believe that under the anointing of God a woman danced on air and came back on the platform unharmed. It is hard for us to believe if we have too much tradition — too much religion — within us.

Imagine what would happen in our churches if we saw a believer appear to be hit with an electrical bolt, get knocked backward fourteen feet, roll under a pew, then get lifted up in mid-air before being sat back to their original position by the Spirit and power of God (Acts 9:3-4; 8:39; Ezekiel 2:2). In these biblical references it was not electricity. It was the Holy Ghost. So there is a scriptural precedent for this type of manifestation.

As we wait on the Lord's return, we shall see more of God's Spirit manifested in ways that will seem strange, unusual and extraordinary. We will see believers come out of dead churches to be where the action of God is evident.

> It came even to pass, as the trumpeters and singers were as one, to make one sound to be heard in praising and thanking the Lord; and when they lifted up their voice with the trumpets and cymbals and instruments of musick, and praised the Lord, saying, For he is good; for his mercy endureth for ever: that then the house was filled with a cloud, even the house of the Lord;
>
> So that the priests could not stand to minister by reason of the cloud: for the glory of the Lord had filled the house of God.
>
> 2 Chronicles 5:13,14

These priests could not stand because of the glory of God that filled the house.

> Now when Solomon had made an end of praying, the fire came down from heaven, and consumed the burnt offering and the sacrifices; and the glory of the Lord filled the house.
>
> And the priests could not enter into the house of the Lord, because the glory of the Lord had filled the Lord's house.
>
> 2 Chronicles 7:1,2

So much glory of God was in the house of the Lord that the priests could not even enter it! The manifestation of God's power was such that the priests could not walk through the door. This cloud was so thick that there was no room for human beings. If the people wanted to have church, they could not because God's glory kept them outside. The next verse tells of the people's response.

> And when all the children of Israel saw how the fire came down, and the glory of the Lord upon the house, they bowed themselves with their faces to the ground upon the pavement, and worshipped, and praised the Lord, saying, For he is good; for his mercy endureth for ever.
>
> 2 Chronicles 7:3

We have more than enough Scripture to give evidence of such differing and unusual manifestations of God's

Spirit. As I said earlier, every great revival throughout the Church age has been accompanied by supernatural signs and wonders.

In the 1700's, John Wesley, founder of the Methodist denomination, was preaching, then the next thing he knew, a woman collapsed and fell on the floor. This was the first time a manifestation such as this ever happened in his ministry. They called two doctors who said, "Her heartbeat seems to be all right, but there is something funny, I mean, it is not normal." They even called a hypnotist to examine her. He said, "She is not hypnotized, but she is in a trance." This hypnotist didn't know how scriptural he was.

> **On the morrow, as they went on their journey, and drew nigh unto the city, Peter went upon the housetop to pray about the sixth hour:**
>
> **And he became very hungry, and would have eaten: but while they made ready, he fell into a trance.**
> **Acts 10:9,10**

This vision from Peter's trance led to the first Holy Spirit baptism of the Gentiles in his time.

When the members of John Wesley's Methodist congregation began to ask about the woman's trance, Wesley said, "I don't know, but we will just wait here and see if she comes to. If it is from the devil, I am sure she will say. And if it is from God, she will say." So, according to Wesley's autobiography, they all sat and watched that dear woman lying there for forty-five minutes.

Can you imagine, they stopped church and were all sitting and watching a perfectly healthy woman who was lying perfectly still! After forty-five minutes passed, both of her arms suddenly shot into the air and she started saying, "Glory to God." Then Wesley got up and said, "It's God! It's God! It's God!" And she began to tell how the Lord had appeared to her in a vision while she was in that condition. All the unbelievers present in that service got saved. Wesley had a lot of sense. That was the first time it happened in his ministry, but thereafter Holy Spirit manifestations continued to happen.

Charles Finney, the greatest revivalist of modern times, lived in the 1800's. It has been said that more of his converts stayed true to the Lord Jesus Christ, percentage wise, then any other minister since the Apostle Paul. When he was in New York, over 400 people went out under the power of God, and he did not touch one of them. They just started falling.

In the 1700s, the great America Awakening revivalist George Whitefield was preaching to such large crowds in Boston, Massachusetts, that some of the people could not see him. So in order to get a better view, they climbed up into trees. But when they did he would say from the podium, "Get out of those trees because when the power of God comes, you are going to fall out of them." I am sure there were skeptics. That is until people began falling down left and right out of the trees. It was reported that in Boston, Massachusetts, seventeen people fell out of trees under the power of God. It was too late to climb down when the Spirit of God manifested.

The Bible says the Spirit of God is like the wind. You cannot see which way the wind is going, but you can see the results of where it has been.

To get a picture of many of the spectacular manifestations of the presence of God, let's look again at the testimony of Sister Etter. Let me quote something from the book, *Signs and Wonders,* about the life of Sister Maria Woodworth-Etter:

"After many invitations from Hartford City and believing that the Spirit of God was leading that way, I consented to go and went believing God would do a great work. I commenced meeting there about the first of January,

1885, in the Methodist church. The first night it was not known if we would be there to commence that evening. They rang the bell and people came from every direction and filled the church to overflowing.

"The church was cold and formal. And many of the best citizens had drifted into skepticism. I knew that it would take a wonderful display of God's power to convince the people, so I prayed for God to display His power that the sinner might know that God still lives and that there is a reality in religion and might convict him of a terrible judgment. Five of the leading members of the church said they would unite with me in prayer for the Lord to pour out the power from on high so the city would be shaken and the country for miles around." (Now, keep in mind, this is the lady under whose ministry horses had gone out under the power of God.)

"We prayed that Christians and sinners might fall as dead men and that the slain of the Lord might be many. And the Lord answered our prayers in a remarkable manner. The class leader's little boy fell under the power of God first. He rose up, stepped on the pulpit, and began to talk with the wisdom and power of God. His father then began to shout and praise the Lord as the little fellow exhorted and asked the people to come to Christ. People began to weep all over the house. Some shouted. Others fell prostrate!

"Diverse operations of the Spirit then began to be seen. This display of the power continued to increase until we closed the meetings which lasted about five weeks. The power of the Lord like the wind swept all over the city up one street and down another, sweeping through the places of business, workshops, saloons, arresting sinners of all classes. The Scriptures were fulfilled. The wicked flee where no man pursueth. Men, women and children were struck down in their homes, in their places of business, on the highway and lay as dead. They had wonderful visions and rose converted, giving glory to God. When they told what they had seen, their faces shone like angels.

"The fear of God fell upon the city. The police said they had never seen such a change and that they had nothing to do. They said they made no arrests and that the power of God seemed to preserve the city. A spirit of love rested over the city. There was no fighting, no swearing on the streets and the people moved softly. (I guess they would!) And that there seemed to be a spirit of love and kindness among all classes as if they felt they were in the presence of God.

"A merchant fell in a trance in his home and laid several hours. Hundreds went in to look at him. He had a vision and a message for the church. The Lord showed him the condition of many of the members. He told part of his vision, but refused to deliver the message to the church and he was then struck dumb. (He could not speak a word because he refused to tell what the Lord wanted him to. It pays to obey.) The Lord showed him he would never speak again until he delivered the message. So he rose to his feet weeping to tell the vision and God loosed his tongue. Those present knew he had been dumb. When he began to talk and tell his experience it had a wonderful effect on the church and sinners.

"One night there was a party seventeen miles from the city. Some of the young ladies thought they would have some fun. They began to mimic and act out the trance. The Lord struck some of them down. They lay there as if they had been shot. Their fun-making was soon turned into prayer meetings and cries of mercy were heard.

"The people came to the meetings in sleigh loads many miles. One night while a sleigh load of men and women were going to the meeting, they were jesting about the trances that were happening. They made the remark to each other that they were going in a trance that night. Before the meeting closed all that were making fun were struck down by the power of God and lay like dead people and had to be taken home on that sled in that condition. Those that came with me were very much frightened when they saw them lying there since they knew how they had been making fun of the power of God on the way to the meeting.

"Scoffers and mockers were stricken down in all parts of the house. One man was mocking a woman of whose body God had taken control. She had been preaching with gestures (like shaking). When in that mocking attitude, God struck him dumb. He became rigid and remained with his hands up and his mouth drawn in that mocking way for five hours — a gazing stock for all in the house.

"The fear of God fell on all. They saw it was a fearful thing to mock God or make fun of His Word. Surely the Lord worked in a wonderful way in this meeting."

The book goes on and on telling of the effects of revival in that particular town.

Another angelic visitation happened in one of those meetings. To quote *Signs and Wonders* again:

"In a meeting in 1915 in Los Angeles, California, a particular person by the name of John, who spoke seven languages, was present. Another brother, Wiley, went out under the power of God, got baptized in the Holy Ghost and got up speaking in Turkish — perfect Turkish. It just so happened this brother, John, who spoke seven languages could understand everything Wiley was saying. Brother John fell on his face and cried to God to have mercy. His heart was broken because of the sinners who could not hear this Turkish voice of God.

"John went home that night. He went to bed and to sleep and he was awakened by a voice and saw two angels standing by his bed. His room was in darkness, but a light filled the room as the angels were bright and shining as the sun. They had long golden hair and beautiful wings which carried a golden palm. Even their hands and feet as well as fingers and toenails were all shining with the same brightness. Their feet never touched the floor, but they stood on a level with the bed. Brother John thought Jesus was coming for sure and tried to awaken the brother who slept with him but he continued sleeping.

"One of the angels spoke to him in such a tender voice of sweetness and said in English the same message that Brother Wiley at church had given in Turkish, which was: 'Now go back and warn God's people to watch and pray, for the time is at hand for the coming of the Lord. Tell them to warn the American people (this is 1915) that God is preaching to Europe at the canon's mouth because He spread His Hand all day long to a rebellious people, speaking to them by the Spirit. Each nation claims its god to be the greatest, yet in reality they are all mocking God. Tell the American people that they are the first nation to receive the baptism of the Holy Spirit and to repent while the windows of heaven are open to pour out the Spirit on all flesh. Tell them the knowledge they profess came from the Nazarene, the Son of God. For the country, before the Gospel came, was evil and full of darkness. But even now, men reject the wisdom of God by making themselves greater than God. A man will come in the future. He will soon conquer Europe, and God will preach to this nation at the mouth of a canon. Those who are asleep or deceived will remain asleep, and those who have their eyes on man will remain with man. And this country will also in that day be conquered by the man of Europe. Then Jesus will catch away His bride, and God will take away His Spirit from the earth. And those who are not filled with the Spirit, whose lamps are not trimmed and burning, will fall on that day. The time is at hand.' The angels then disappeared softly with smiles through the wall."

Believers know that Antichrist will one day rise up from the Commonwealth of Europe, but God is still on the throne. The more we reach for the heavenly throne, the more that throne takes up residency in our hearts and in our midst. The more the glory of God is manifested, the more people will be filled with His Spirit. And to be filled with the Spirit always begins with speaking in tongues.

I am looking for the day when everyone sees the angels of God in church services. Angels are not given to preaching the Gospel, but they can tell us things God wants us to know (Acts 8:26; 10:3-5; 12:7-8; 27:23-25). We should be looking for the supernatural to be poured out in greater measure.

We can keep the supernatural flowing by staying in faith and fervent in Spirit. We cannot afford to get too religious or dignified. I don't think Saul was considered "dignified" as he laid there flat on his face on the Damascus road in front of his companions who were arresting Christians. And it was this very same man who went on to write two-thirds of the New Testament. He had visions, trances, angelic visitations, and even Jesus appeared to him supernaturally.

If you desire to have more of God's Spirit, the Holy Spirit, manifested in your life, pray with me now:

Father, I thank You for the depth of You that is available to me. I ask You to baptize me now in your Holy Spirit. I pray for the initial evidence of the baptism of the Holy Spirit that leads to the other eight gifts of your Holy Spirit, the gift of tongues. Baptize me now. And I ask You to lead and minister to me in the days ahead like never before. I yield myself to You and to Your ministry of supernatural workings. Father, let Your ministering spirits be with me. I believe angels are encamped around those who fear You to keep away the onslaughts of the enemy. So Father, let angels also come and speak to me and the rest of Your children, because they are ministering servants sent forth to minister to the heirs of salvation. Father, I promise to keep my eyes upon You. I promise to look to Jesus as my source and as the Shepherd of the Church. In Jesus' name I pray, Amen.

Additional copies of this book and other book titles
from **ALBURY PUBLISHING** are
available at your local bookstore.

Albury Publishing
P.O. Box 470406
Tulsa, Oklahoma 74147-0406

Albury Publishing